CW01023406

The Structural Crisis *of* Capital

WORKS BY THE SAME AUTHOR

Satire and Reality, 1955

La rivolta degli intellettuali in Ungheria, 1958

Attila József e l'arte moderna, 1964

Marx's Theory of Alienation, 1970

The Necessity of Social Control, 1971

Aspects of History and Class Consciousness, ed., 1971

Lukács's Concept of Dialectic, 1972

Neocolonial Identity and Counter-Consciousness, ed., 1978

The Work of Sartre: Search for Freedom, 1979

Philosophy, Ideology and Social Science, 1986

The Power of Ideology, 1989

Beyond Capital, 1995

L'Alternativa alla Società del Capitale, 2000

Socialism or Barbarism, 2001

A educação para além do capital, 2005

O desafio e o fardo do tempo histórico, 2007

The Challenge and Burden of Historical Time, 2008

The Structural Crisis *of* Capital

by ISTVÁN MÉSZÁROS

MONTHLY REVIEW PRESS
New York

Copyright © 2010 by István Mészáros

All rights reserved

Library of Congress Cataloging-in-Publication Data

Mészáros, István.

  The structural crisis of capital /István Mészáros.

    p. cm.

  Includes bibliographical references.

  ISBN 978-1-58367-208-2 (pbk.) — ISBN 978-1-58367-209-9 (cloth)

  1. Capitalism. I. Title.

  HB501.M622515 2009

  330.12'2—dc22

                            2009023587

Monthly Review Press

146 West 29th Street, Suite 6w

New York, NY 10001

5 4 3 2 1

Contents

For Donatella; and for the people of
Brazil's Landless Workers Movement (MST)
whose struggle for emancipation she admired and supported.

Foreword

by John Bellamy Foster

If I were asked to sum up the significance of István Mészáros for our time in a phrase I would have to follow President Hugo Chávez of Venezuela in referring to him as the "Pathfinder of Socialism."[1] His work, in such writings as *Marx's Theory of Alienation* (1970), *The Power of Ideology* (1989), *Beyond Capital* (1995), *The Challenge and Burden of Historical Time* (2008), *The Structural Crisis of Capital*—the book before you (2009), and *Social Structure and Forms of Consciousness* (forthcoming, 2010), provides a strategic vision of the building of socialism, the absence of which for many decades constituted one of the principal weaknesses of the anti-capitalist movement worldwide. For Mészáros "the structural crisis of capital" arises not simply from the fact that the system is now face to face for the first time with its own "absolute limits," but also from the reality that the necessary conditions of a mass-based, hegemonic socialist alternative are emerging, providing the bases of a new revolutionary situation globally. The depth and breadth of his critique of the capital system—extending to post-capitalist regimes like the Soviet Union—offers a powerful set of insights into the historical necessity of socialism, and this in turn informs his critique of capital itself, constituting a single strategic argument. As Chávez has stated, the importance of Mészáros's magnum opus *Beyond Capital* is to be found in its "subtitle: 'Toward a Theory of Transition.' It is a theoretical effort, because Karl Marx did not develop a theory of transition."[2]

The immediate context in which Mészáros's *Structural Crisis of Capital* appears is what is commonly and euphemistically known as the Great Recession, or the immense financial and economic crisis in which we are now engulfed, manifesting itself on a scale not seen since the Great Depression of the 1930s.[3] Mészáros begins and ends his book with the current economic malaise. But he explains this as part of a wider disjuncture stretching back to the early 1970s.[4] This structural crisis cannot be seen simply in narrow economic terms. Rather it also encompasses the global ecological crisis; what Mészáros calls "the potentially deadliest form of global hegemonic imperialism" (179); and the manifold social and cultural contradictions emanating from the hierarchical power relations of the prevailing order. "The epochal *structural crisis* of the capital system," moreover, transcends all merely "*cyclic and conjunctural* economic crises…affecting *all conceivable forms of the capital system as such*, not only capitalism," asserting itself through the activation of "*the absolute limits of capital as a mode of social metabolic reproduction*." This poses dangers "incomparably more severe than even the Great World Economic Crisis of 1929-1933," due to the "truly global character" of the world crisis this time around (172).

So dialectically interconnected, in Mészáros's conception, are capital's deepening structural crisis and the imperative of a genuine socialist transition that it is impossible to address the former without also addressing the latter. His critique of *capital* (as opposed to capitalism) is equally a critique of the early "socialist" (or post-capitalist) experiments, which in failing to eradicate the capital relation in its entirety, but merely mediating this via the state, ended up in a historical dead end—while nevertheless illuminating the path that the socialism of the twenty-first century must take. In Mészáros's analysis this path can be summed up as: "substantive equality," "self-critique," and communal self-organization of productive relations, which taken together define a sustainable socialist society.[5]

Mészáros strongly counsels against the *defensive*, purely economistic orientation of laborist and social democratic movements, which, faced with the default of capital, do everything they can to bail it out and restore the very economic power that keeps them and the entire working class in subservience. Rather it is essential, he argues, to take full *offensive* advantage of the current weakness of capital as a system of social metabolic reproduction to alter the rules of the game fundamentally and irrevocably *by political means.* Opposing those who claim that the working class has been integrated into the system, he makes it clear that this is a systemic impossibility even in the wealthiest capitalist states, and at most extends to the trade union leadership (190-95). The working class remains everywhere an alienated power, the indispensable agent of *potential* revolutionary change. Still, in responding to the question of whether such a revolutionary transformation will actually take place, Mészáros answers bluntly: "It depends" (p. 187). Genuine human emancipation, altering society "from top to bottom," in Marx's terms, can only be brought about through unrelenting struggle and hence is a contingent aspect of history (85).

The structural crisis of capital, described in this book, has been worsening for decades and has now reached a point where it has taken on real urgency in every region of the globe. Critics of the system can therefore no longer hide behind the comforting illusion that socialism will eventually arise of its own accord, or that the world can simply afford to wait. In this respect Chávez (quoted in Chapter Five "Bolívar and Chávez") declared before the World Social Forum in Caracas in January 2006: that to limit anti-systemic activities to an annual *"touristic/folkloric encounter would be terrible, because we would be simply wasting time, and we have no time to waste.* I believe that it is not given to us to speak in terms of future centuries...we have no time to waste; the challenge is to save the conditions of life on this planet, to save the human species, to change the course of history, to change the world" (p. 136).

The out-of-control destruction that now characterizes the capital system on a world scale, and imperils all life on the planet, has its dialectical antithesis in the potential for an acceleration of history, through the activation of a genuine, mass-based revolutionary struggle for substantive equality. The conservative nineteenth-century cultural historian Jacob Burckhardt, looking back on an earlier era of revolution, once described a "historical crisis" as a time in which "a crisis in the whole state of things is produced, involving whole epochs and all or many peoples of the same civilization. . . . The historical process is suddenly accelerated in terrifying fashion. Developments which otherwise take centuries seem to flit by like phantoms in months or weeks, and are fulfilled."[6] Today the structural crisis of capital provides the historical setting for a new revolutionary movement for social emancipation in which developments normally taking centuries would flit by like phantoms in decades or even years. But the force for such necessary, vital change remains with the people themselves, and rests on humanity's willingness to constitute itself as both subject and object of history, through the collective struggle to create a just and sustainable world. This, Mészáros insists, constitutes the unprecedented challenge and burden of *our* historical time.

The Substance of the Crisis[1]
by Richard Antunes

I.

Much has been written about the crisis. A crisis of subprime mortgages, a crisis of speculation, a banking crisis, a financial crisis, a global crisis, a rerun of the crisis of 1929, and so forth. A phenomenology of crises has blossomed, and what was said yesterday is obsolete today. The major periodicals—*The Economist* for one—speak of a "crisis of confidence" and the catchphrase spreads. The crisis as an act of volition. *Fiducia!*, the Latins would say. That is the key to analysis.

The governments of the countries in crisis, in the United States, Europe, and many other corners of the world, seem to have rediscovered *full-blown privatized statism* as the recipe for curtailing the crisis of "confidence." The neo-Keynesian solutions, buried for the last four decades, and considered one of the main evils of earlier crises of capitalism, has reemerged as the salvation from the *true way to servitude*; that is, mankind's subjection to the designs of the destructive logic of capitalism and, in particular, its hegemonic financial center.

Beyond the phenomenology of the crisis, we could recall several critical authors from the left who have tried to go beyond the surface and uncover the structural and systemic fundamentals of the melting and liquefying of the capital system.

Robert Kurz, for example, has been warning us since the early 1990s that the crisis that bankrupted countries in the so-called "real socialism" camp (with the USSR at the front) and also devastated the "Third World" was the expression of a crisis in the *mode of commodity production* that would later migrate to the heart of the capitalist system.

François Chesnais highlighted the complex connections between production, financialization ("the most fetishized form of accumulation"), and capitalist globalization, emphasizing that the financial sphere feeds on the wealth generated by investment and the exploitation of a trained workforce worldwide. And it is a part of that wealth, channeled toward the financial sphere, that inflates flaccid, fictitious capital.

But István Mészáros, since the late sixties, has been systematically exposing the *crisis* that was already beginning to devastate the global capital system, pointing out that the 1968 rebellions and the monumental restructuring of capital in 1973, were harbingers of a substantial change outlined in both the capitalist and the global systems of capital.[2]

He wrote that the capital system (and the capitalist system in particular), after living through an era of cycles, was entering a new, never-before-seen phase of *structural crisis characterized by a depressed continuum* that would confine the previous cyclical phase to history. Although there would be changes in the epicenters, the crisis has shown itself to be enduring, systemic, and structural.

What is more, it has shown the failure of the two most daring state systems of control and regulation of capital seen in the twentieth century. The first, of a Keynesian type, was typical of *welfare state* capitalist societies. The second, of a "Soviet type" (established, according to Mészáros, in the Soviet Union and other "post-capitalist" societies), resulted from a social revolution that tried to destroy capital and was devoured by it. In both instances, the political entity charged with regulation was deregulated at the end of a long period, by the very system of social metabolism of capital.[3] A similar process seems to be taking place in China today, making it an exceptional laboratory for critical thinking.

II.

This book is a condensation of a number of articles and interviews presenting the main theses and formulations in the work of István Mészáros, written over more than three decades and now published in a single volume, summarizing some of his stronger theses at a decisive time in the twenty-first century when *all that seemed solid melts into air, with capitalism undergoing a strong process of liquefaction.*

The sum total of resources, trillions of dollars destroyed in the last few months, is in itself overwhelming. The crisis in the global financial system, and the reduction of industrial, agricultural, and services output, are all too evident. Since 1929, capitalism has not seen so deep a crisis, one that surfaces even in the discourse of capital holders, their managers, and political lieutenants. In recent decades, István Mészáros has been one of the densest, deepest, most qualified, and most radical of critics. This book is an example of the compelling force and weight of his vast and powerful corpus of works.

If I could condense into a few pages some of the theses that define the current *structural crisis of capital,* I would begin by saying that Mészáros makes a devastating criticism of the workings characteristic of its *socio-metabolic system.*

His penetrating research, covering all of the twentieth century, has led him to the conclusion that, having *no limits to its expansion,* the system of capital ends up as a *destructive* and deeply *uncontrollable* process. it is made up of what he, following Marx, calls *second-order mediations*—when everything becomes controlled by the logic of capital's valorization process, with no regard for vital human and social imperatives. Superfluous production and consumerism corrode labor, with the correlation of more precarious employment and structural unemployment, as well as a level of destruction of nature never before seen on such a global scale.

Expansionist in its unlimited and growing quest for surplus value, *destructive* in its development characterized by the pursuit of superfluity and waste, the capital system becomes uncontrollable when it reaches its outer limits. All that, concisely stated here, means that, after a long period of cycles, the crisis, still according to Mészáros, has taken the shape of an *endemic, cumulative, chronic, permanent crisis,* which confronts us again as a vital imperative of our time, given the specter of global destruction, the task of creating a social alternative for building a *new mode of production* and a *new way of life,* one firmly and openly opposed to the destructive logic of the capitalist system dominant today.

Therefore, unlike the cycles of expansion that have shaped capitalism throughout its history, alternating periods of expansion and crisis, since the 1960s and 1970s, we find ourselves immersed in what Mészáros has called a *depressed continuum* showing the characteristics of a *structural crisis.*

His analysis already forewarned that within the capitalist countries of the center, "crisis management" mechanisms would become ever more recurrent—and ever more inadequate—once the radical gulf between *production for social needs and self-reproduction of capital changed the character of modern capitalism, with devastating consequences for mankind.*

Given the new *form of being* of the crisis, we have thus entered a new period characterized not by cyclical interval of expansion and recession, but rather *more frequent and longer lasting precipitations.* Since this is a crisis of the very realization of value, the destructive logic that accelerates in our days has enabled Mészáros to develop another thesis: that the system of capital can no longer develop without using the *decreasing rate of utilization of use-value of commodities* as an intrinsic mechanism. This happens because capital does not distinguish between *use-value* (as relating to the sphere of needs) and *exchange-value* (as relating to the valorization of value). On the contrary, it radically subordinates the former to the latter.

This means, the author adds, that the utilization of commodities can vary from one extreme to the other, from having their use-value immediately realized to never being used, without ever losing their essential usefulness to capital. And, given that the *diminishing trend of utilization* drastically reduces the useful life of commodities—a *sine qua non* for the proper functioning of the valorization process in its reproductive cycle— that diminishing trend becomes one of the main mechanisms through which capital can accomplish its accumulation, by destroying the useful life of commodities and the subordination of use-value to the imperatives of exchange-value.

The widening gulf between production truly dedicated to meeting human needs and production dedicated to the self-reproduction of capital intensifies the destructive side effects, of which the two mentioned above put the present and future of our species at risk: the structural precariousness of labor and the destruction of nature. Mészáros's conclusion is forceful: even if 90 percent of the material and labor resources needed for the production and distribution of a given commodity (for example, a cosmetic product) went directly to the trash can, and only 10 percent were actually used in making the product, for the real or imaginary benefit of the consumer, the obviously devastating practices involved would be completely justified under the criteria of capitalist "efficiency," "rationality," and "economy," due to the proven profitability of the product. And, he adds, what would become of humankind when 5 percent of the world's population (the United States) consumes 25 percent of all available energy resources? And what if the other 95 percent engaged in a similar level of consumption? The current tragedy of environmental destruction in China is emblematic.

This underlines another fundamental contradiction in which the world has been more deeply sunk since the beginning of the century: if unemployment rates continue to rise, the levels of social degradation and barbarism intrinsic to unemployment will spiral too. If, on the other hand, the world resumes its former rate of growth again, increasing production and the way of life founded on superfluity and waste, we shall see an even higher rate of nature's destruction, intensifying the destructive logic now dominant.

This situation of *systemic and structural crisis* has another central component, the corrosion of labor. After the worsening of the crisis in the United States and other central capitalist countries, we have seen deep repercussions on a global scale in the sphere of labor. Amid the hurricane now battering the heart of the capitalist system, we see the erosion of relatively regulated and contracted labor, heir to the Taylorist and Fordist eras, which was the norm in the twentieth century—the result of a century of workers' struggles for social rights. This is now being replaced by several forms of "entrepreneurship," "cooperativism," "voluntary work," and "atypical labor." These formats range from the super-exploitation of labor to self-exploitation, always in the direction of a structurally greater precarization of the labor force on a global scale. And, of course, there is an explosion of unemployment affecting enormous numbers of workers, be they men or women, permanent or precarized, formal or informal, native-born or immigrant, the latter being the first to be harshly penalized.[4]

In a recent report, the International Labor Organization (ILO), using fairly moderate data, forecast the loss of fifty million jobs in 2009. It would only take one large carmaker in the United States closing its doors to create further millions of unemployed. The newspapers in Europe report every day on thousands of workers losing their jobs.

The same ILO report adds that almost 1.5 billion workers will see their salaries cut and unemployment spreading in the same period.[5] But it is a well-established fact that international statistics on employment fail to detect *hidden unemployment*, often absent from official statistics. And, as Mészáros often points out, if real statistics on unemployment in India and China were included, the numbers would grow many times over.

It is worth pointing out that in China, twenty-six million former rural workers who had found work in cities have lost it in the last months of 2008 and the first months of 2009, and can no longer find available work in the countryside, thus triggering a new wave of revolts in that country. In Latin America, the ILO adds that "up to 2.4 million people could swell the ranks of the unemployed in the region during 2009," adding to the almost sixteen million already unemployed.[6]

In the United States, Great Britain, and Japan, unemployment rates in the first few months of 2009 are the highest in decades. That is why businessmen the world over are pressing for new legislation to make labor laws more flexible, using the fallacy that this is a way of saving jobs. It has been already tried in the Unied States, Great Britain, Spain, and Argentina in a very intense way, but unemployment has just kept on spiraling upward.

Therefore, taking a completely different tack from those who confine the crisis to the world of banking, a "crisis of the financial system," or a "credit crunch," for Mészáros, "the enormous speculative expansion of financial adventurism—particularly in the last three or four decades—is by its nature inseparable from *a deepening of the crisis in the productive branches of industry* as well as from the ensuing troubles arising from the utterly sluggish capital accumulation (and indeed failed accumulation) in the productive field of the economy. Now, inevitably, in the field of industrial production the crisis is getting much worse. Naturally, the necessary consequence of the ever deepening crisis in the productive branches of the 'real economy' . . . is the growth of unemployment everywhere on a frightening scale, and of the human misery associated with it. To expect a happy solution to these problems from the capitalist state's rescue operations would be a great illusion."

And he adds: "the recent attempts to counter the intensifying crisis symptoms, by the cynically camouflaged nationalization of astronomic magnitudes of capitalist bankruptcy, out of the yet to be invented state resources, could only highlight the deep-seated antagonistic causal determinations of the capital system's destructiveness. For what is fundamentally at stake today is not simply a massive financial crisis but humanity's potential self-destruction at this juncture of historical development, both militarily and through the ongoing destruction of nature."

If capital's answer to its structural crisis is the neo-Keynesianism of the fully privatized state, the answer from the social forces of labor must be radical. Against the fallacy of the neo-Keynesian "alternative," always welcomed by those on the "left" acting to promote "Order"—"alternatives" are fated to fail. As demonstrated by Mészáros in his analysis of the twentieth century, they constitute the *line of least resistance to capital.* The necessary challenge was already indicated in his article, "Radical Politics and Transition to Socialism."[7] A shorter version of this article was delivered as a lecture in Athens in April 1983. The article is reprinted in full in Part IV of his *Beyond Capital.* In it, he already made the distinction between *structural and systemic crises* and the *cyclic or conjunctural* crises of the past, as well as the need for radical politics in opposition to the (neo-) Keynesian alternatives that capital adopts in its moments of crisis.

It is worth remembering a recent *Notes from the Editors* in *Monthly Review* that points to Mészáros's decisive contribution: "How is the left to react to the economic crisis and to such attempts to socialize losses on the back of the population as a whole? Should we in the face of a depression and financial crisis be offering our own, slightly more benign strategies for saving the system?"

The Note adds: "In September (2008) some progressives in the United States argued that it was necessary to support Paulson's 'bailout the rich' plan lest there be a depression. Three months later we have trillions in government funds handed over to the richest people on the planet *and* a depression. The crucial point, in our view, was captured by Mészáros in *Beyond Capital* where he explained that "radical politics can only accelerate its own demise . . . if it consents to define its own scope in terms of limited economic targets which are in fact necessarily dictated by the established socioeconomic structure in crisis."[8]

As Mészáros wrote in his prophetic 1982 article:

> Since the *immediate* manifestations of the crisis are *economic*—from inflation to unemployment, and from the bankruptcy of local industrial and commercial enterprises to a general trade-war and the potential collapse of the international financial system—the pressure emanating from the given social base inevitably tends to define the task at hand in terms of finding urgent *economic* answers at the level of the crisis-manifestations themselves, while leaving their *social causes* intact.

And, he went on:

> 'belt tightening' and 'accepting sacrifices needed' to 'creating real jobs,' 'injecting new investment funds', 'increasing productivity and competitiveness,' etc.—imposes the *social premises* of the established order (in the name of purely *economic* imperatives) over the socialist political initiative . . . within the framework of the old social premises and structural determinations, thereby ending up with the revitalization of capital.

This explains why for Mészáros any attempt to overcome that system of social metabolism that follows the *line of least resistance* to capital and confines itself to the *institutional and parliamentary* sphere, is doomed to failure. Only a radical extraparliamentary policy that drastically reorients the economic structure could destroy capital's system of social domination and its destructive logic.

To create a *mode of production and living* fundamentally different from the current one is, therefore, a vital challenge launched by Mészáros.

Now at the start of the twenty-first century, building a new meaningful way of life reinstates the imperative to establish a new system of social metabolism, a new mode of production based on *self-determined activity*, i.e. based on the activity of *freely associated individuals* (Marx), driven by the need *to go beyond capital*. Contrary to production based on *surplus time* in the service of exchange value for reproducing capital, it becomes vital to engage in activities based on *disposable time* dedicated to the production of socially useful goods corresponding to real needs.

Under capitalism (and capital too) the *use-value of socially needed goods became subordinated to their exchange-value*, which dominated the logic of the system of production. Basic productive and reproductive functions were radically split between those who *produce* (the workers) and those who *control* (the capitalists and their managers). Having been the first mode of production to create a logic that does not give priority to the real needs of society, capital, according to Mészáros, established a system dedicated to its own self-valorization, *independent from the real self-reproductive needs of humankind*.

As a counterpoint, a new kind of society will only make sense and be truly emancipated if its vital functions—those that control its system of social metabolism—*are effectively exercised autonomously by the freely associated producers and not by an external, extraneous body in control of those functions*.

The main contribution of this small but powerful book by István Mészáros is the revelation of the deepest meanings of the *current crisis, its global, structural, and systemic sense*, and its devastatingly destructive character. It must be read by all those men and women that in any way have to confront the dominant system of social metabolism, essentially destructive to humankind and nature, in their social and day-to-day struggles. Reading it will help us to reflect, imagine, and conceive another form of truly socialist sociability capable of rescuing the real meaning of production and reproduction of human life and, thus, of aiding the creation of the essential critical conditions for the blossoming of a new authentic and emancipated sociability that would constitute a great adancement in the twenty-first century. It would be in the best spirit of the work of Mészáros and his ardent and impassioned defense of humankind.

CHAPTER ONE

The Unfolding Crisis and the Relevance of Marx[1]

Some of you may have been present at our meeting, in May of this year, when I recalled what I said to Lucien Goldman in Paris a few months before France's historic May 1968. In contrast to the then-prevailing perspective of "organized capitalism," which was supposed to have successfully left behind the stage of "crisis capitalism"—a view prominently asserted by Herbert Marcuse and shared also by my dear friend Lucien Goldman—I insisted that, compared to the crisis we are actually heading for, the Great World Economic Crisis of 1929-1933 would look like the Vicar's tea party.

In the last few weeks you have had a foretaste of what I had in mind, but no more than a foretaste. The structural crisis of the capital system as a whole, which we are experiencing in our time on an epochal scale, is bound to get considerably worse. It will become in due course much deeper, in the sense of invading not only the world of more or less parasitic global finance but also every single domain of our social, economic, and cultural life.

The obvious question we must now address concerns the nature of the globally unfolding crisis and the conditions required for its feasible resolution.

1. "CONFIDENCE" AND ITS DISAPPEARANCE

If you try to remember what you have heard endlessly repeated about the current crisis, one word stands out, overshadowing all of the other claimed diagnoses and corresponding remedies. That word is *confidence*. If we could get a ten pound note for every occasion when that magic word has been offered for public consumption in the last two weeks all over the world, not to mention its continued reassertion ever since, we would all be millionaires. Our only problem would be what to do with our suddenly acquired millions. For none of our banks, not even our recently nationalized banks—nationalized to the tune of no less than two-thirds of their capital assets—could supply the legendary confidence required for safe deposit or investment.

Our Prime Minister, Gordon Brown, presented us with the memorable phrase: "Confidence is the most precious thing." I know the song—and probably most of us do—which tells us that: "Love is the most precious thing." But *confidence* in capitalist banking being the most precious thing—that suggestion is utterly perverse! Nevertheless, the advocacy of this magic remedy now seems to be universal. It is repeated as if confidence could simply rain out of the sky or grow on trees.

Three days ago (on the 18th of October) the BBC's flagship Sunday morning interview program, the Andrew Marr program, wheeled out a very distinguished elderly gentleman: Sir Brian Pitman, the former head of Lloyds Bank. They did not say when he headed that organization, but the way he spoke made it amply clear. For it transpired through his respectfully received answers that he might have been the head of Lloyds Bank well before the world economic crisis of 1929–33. He introduced a great conceptual innovation into the confidence discourse, saying that our troubles were all due to some *over*confidence. And he immediately also demonstrated the meaning of "overconfidence," by saying that there can be no serious problem today because the market always takes care of everything. Even if sometimes it has gone unexpectedly far down, later it always goes up again. So it will do so this time, and it will unfailingly go up again and again in the future. The present crisis should not be exaggerated, he said, because it is much less serious today than what we experienced way back in 1974. For in 1974 we had a three-day working week in Britain [introduced by the Conservative government to save energy during the miners' strikes], and now we do not have it. And who could argue with that irrefutable fact?

2. A PSEUDO-HEGELIAN TRIAD

Thus, we now have the magic explanatory word of all our troubles not standing like an unhappy orphan, alone, but as part of something like a Fukuyamized pseudo-Hegelian triad: *confidence, lack of confidence*, and *overconfidence*. The only constituent missing from this magic explanatory discourse is the real foundation of our perilous banking and insurance system, which operates on the ground of self-serving *confidence tricks* that sooner or later are bound to be (and from time to time actually have been) found out.

In any case, all this talk about the absolute virtue of confidence in capitalist economic management is much like the explanation offered in Indian mythology about the supporting ground of the universe. In that ancient vision of the world, it is said that the universe is carried, most reassuringly, on the back of an elephant. No one should think of that as a difficulty. For the elephant is, even more reassuringly, supported on the back of the cosmic tortoise. But what holds up the cosmic tortoise? Don't you dare ask such a question, lest you might be fed to the tigers of Bengal!

Luckily, perhaps, *The Economist* is a little bit more realistic in its assessment of the situation. In the context of our painful subject, the now-acknowledged worsening economic crisis, I am going to give you exact quotations, including some damning figures of capitalist failures that are no longer deniable, taken mainly from such well established and unabashedly class-conscious bourgeois newspapers as *The Economist* and *The Sunday Times*. I will quote them meticulously, word for word, not only because they are prominent in their field but also in order to forestall any accusation of left-wing bias and distortion.

Marx used to say that on the pages of *The Economist* the ruling class is "talking to itself." Things have changed somewhat since those days. For now, even in the specialized field of economic expertise, the ruling class needs a mass circulation propaganda organ for the purpose of general mystification. In Marx's lifetime, the ruling class had plenty of "confidence" and also a great deal of unchallenged "overconfidence." But, under the present circumstances, *The Economist*—the self-righteous mouthpiece of the U.S.-dominated annual "Davos Jamboree"—concedes that the crisis we are facing today is concerned with the difficulties of "Saving the System," according to the cover of its October 11, 2008 issue.

We can grant, of course, that nothing less than 'saving the system' (or not) is what happens to be at stake in our time, even if *The Economist*'s discussion of this problem is rather strange and contradictory. For in its usual way of trying to present its highly partisan position as an objectively balanced view, by using the formula of "on the one hand, but on the other hand," *The Economist* always succeeds in reaching its desired conclusion in favor of the established order. Thus, *The Economist* asserts, in the principal lead article in its October 11 issue, that: "This week saw the first glimmer of a comprehensive global answer to the *confidence gap.*" Now, thankfully, the confidence gap, although reprehensible in itself, is expected to be remedied. This is all thanks to a somewhat mysterious 'comprehensive global answer.'

More realistically, the London weekly also acknowledges in the same editorial article that: "The damage to the real economy is becoming apparent. In America consumer credit is now shrinking, and around *150,000 Americans lost their jobs in September,* the most since 2003. Some industries are hurting badly: car sales are at their lowest level for 16 years as would-be buyers are unable to get credit. General Motors has temporarily shut some of its factories in Europe. Across the globe forward-looking indicators, such as surveys of purchasing managers, are horribly gloomy." They do not say, though, that the confidence gap may have something to do with such facts.

Of course, an apology for the system must prevail in every article, even if it must be presented as the unquestionable word of pragmatic wisdom. In this sense, "saving the system" amounts to the journal's totally uncritical identification with, and the uncontestable advocacy of, an unlimited economic rescue operation—to be accomplished by no means out of the customarily and dogmatically glorified market resources—in favor of the troubled capitalist system. Thus, even the most cherished and well-tried propaganda tenets (of a not only nonexistent but never in reality existent free market) can be now thrown overboard for the noble cause of "saving the system." Accordingly, we are told by *The Economist* that: "The world economy is plainly in a poor shape, but it could get a lot worse. This is the time to put *dogma and politics* to one side and concentrate on *pragmatic answers*. That means *more government intervention* and co-operation in the *short* term than *taxpayers, politicians or indeed free-market newspapers would normally like*."[2]

President George W. Bush has treated us to similar sermons. He told his television audience that normally and instinctively he is a believer in, and a passionate supporter of, the free market, but under the present exceptional circumstances he must think of other ways. He must begin to think under these exceptional circumstances, full stop. You cannot say that you have not been warned.

The sums involved in the recommended "pragmatic" solution, which advocates sweeping aside the "normal likings" of the "taxpayers and free market newspapers" (that is, the now advocated solution that means, in truth, the necessary submission of the great masses of the people to increasing tax burdens sooner or later) are literally astronomical. To quote *The Economist* again: "In little more than three weeks America's government, all told, expanded its gross liabilities by more than $1 trillion—almost twice as much as the cost so far of the Iraq War."[3] "American and European banks will shed some $10 trillions of dollars."[4] "But history teaches an important lesson: that big banking crises are ultimately solved by throwing in large dollops of public money."[5]

Tens of trillions of dollars of public money thrown in and justified in the name of the claimed important lesson of history, and of course in the service of the unchallengeable good cause of saving the system—that is certainly quite a *dollop*. No High Street ice-cream vendor could ever dream about such tsunami-size dollops. Not even in his worst nightmare.

In the course of last year alone, "*The Economist's* food price index jumped by nearly 55%,"[6] and "the food-price spike in late 2007 and early 2008 caused riots in some 30 countries."[7] Such facts reveal even more about the nature of the system, which now finds itself in ever deepening crisis. Can you think of a stronger indictment for a purportedly unsurpassable system of economic production and societal reproduction? At the height of its productive power, this system is producing a global food crisis and the suffering of countless millions all over the world. That is the nature of the system that is expected to be saved now at all costs.

How can one make some tangible sense out of all of the wasted trillions? Since we are talking about *astronomical* magnitudes, I addressed this question to a close friend who is a professor of astrophysics at London University. His answer was that I should point out that *one trillion* alone is roughly *one hundred times the age of our universe.* Now, the official figure for the American debt, which is regularly understated, amounts to more than ten trillion dollars. That is, *one thousand times* the age of our universe.

Let me quote a short passage from a Japanese publication. It reads:

> How much speculative money is moving around the world? According to a Mitsubishi UFJ Securities analysis, the size of the global "real economy," in which goods and services are produced and traded, is estimated at $48.1 trillion. . . . On the other hand, the size of the global "financial economy," the total amount of stocks, securities, and deposits, adds up to $151.8 trillion. The financial economy thus has swollen to more than three times the size of the real economy, growing especially rapidly during the past two decades. The gap is as large as $100 trillion. An analyst involved in this estimation said that about half the amount, $50 trillion is scarcely necessary for the real economy. Fifty trillion dollars are worth well over 5,000 trillion yen, too big a number for me to actually comprehend.[8]

It is, indeed, very difficult even to comprehend, not to mention to justify, as our capital-apologetic politicians and bankers do, the astronomical sums of parasitic speculation accumulated to a magnitude corresponding to 500,000 times the age of our universe. If you wish to have another measure about the magnitude involved, just imagine an unlucky accountant from Roman times, who is asked nothing more than simply to chalk up on his blackboard the figure of 5,000 trillion yen, in Roman numerals. He would be in total despair. He simply could not do it. And even if he had at his disposal Arabic numerals, he would have needed as many as seventeen zeros after the number five in order to write down the figure in question.

The trouble is, though, that our well-heeled politicians and bankers seem to think only of the zeros, and not of their substantive linkages, when they present these problems for public consumption. And that approach cannot work indefinitely. One needs much more than zeros for getting out of the bottomless hole of the global indebtedness to which we are condemned by the system that they now want to save at all costs.

As a matter of fact, Gordon Brown's newfound popularity has a great deal to do with zeros in more ways than one. His astonishing new popularity—which might well turn out to be rather ephemeral—was illustrated last week by the front-page newspaper headline: "*From Zero to Hero.*" The article in question suggested that our Prime Minister actually succeeded in saving the system. That is how he earned the high acclaim.

3. THE NATIONALIZATION OF CAPITALIST BANKRUPTCY

The reason why he was hailed in that way, as a hero, was because he invented a new variety of nationalizing capitalist bankruptcy, to be adopted with untroubled "free market conscience" by other countries as well. That made even George W. Bush feel less guilty about acting against his own proclaimed "passionate instinct" when he nationalized a huge dollop of U.S. capitalist bankruptcy, one single item of which—the liabilities of the giant mortgage companies of Fannie Mae and Freddie Mac—amounted to $5.4 *trillion* (that is to say, the sum required for eleven years of running the Iraq War).

The "pragmatic novelty"—as opposed to "dogma and politics" in the words of *The Economist*—of the recent nationalization of capitalist bankruptcy by New Labour is that the taxpayers get *absolutely nothing* (in other words, zero-zero-zero, as many times as you would like to write it down) for the immense sums of money invested in failed capitalist assets, including our two-thirds nationalized British banks. This kind of nationalization of capitalist bankruptcy is somewhat different from the earlier versions instituted after the Second World War when the Labour Party's Clause 4—advocating the public control of the means of production—was still part of its Constitution. In 1945, the bankrupt sectors of the capitalist economy that were nationalized were transferred to state control. They were generously fattened up again from general taxation for the purpose of proper "privatization" in due course.

Even Conservative Prime Minister Edward Heath's 1971 nationalization of the bankrupt Rolls Royce Company followed the same embarrassing pattern of state controlled and openly admitted nationalization. In our own day, however, the beauty of Gordon Brown's solution is that it removes the embarrassment while multiplying manifold the billions invested in capitalist bankruptcy. Surely, that fully deserves his promotion "from zero to hero" as well as the highest accolade, "Saviour of the World," conferred upon him by some other newspapers. All of this on account of Brown being satisfied with absolute zero in exchange for *our*— not *his*—generously dispensed billions. But can this kind of governmental remedy be considered a lasting solution to our problems, even on a short-term basis? Only a fool could believe that.

In truth, the recent measures adopted by our political and financial authorities only attended to one single aspect of the current crisis: the *liquidity* of the banks, mortgage, and insurance companies. And even that only to a very limited extent. In reality, the huge dollops thrown in represent no more than putting down a deposit, so to speak. Much more will be required in the future, as even the still unfolding disturbances on the world's stock exchanges make clear.

However, well beyond the problem of *liquidity,* another dimension of the financial crisis concerns the near catastrophic *insolvency* of banks and insurance companies. This fact becomes clear once their *liabilities,* assumed through irresponsible speculation, are actually taken into account. To give you just one example: two of our big banks in Britain have liabilities amounting to $2.4 trillion each, acquired on the reckless assumption that they will never have to be met. Can the capitalist state successfully bail them out? Where could the state possibly borrow enough money for such a rescue operation? And what would be the necessary inflationary consequences of simply printing the money in the absence of other solutions?

Moreover, the problems are by no means exhausted by the perilous state of the financial sector. For even more intractably, the productive sectors of capitalist industry are also in serious trouble, no matter how highly developed and favored they might appear to be by their advantageous competitive position in the global pecking order of transnational capital. Due to our limited time, I must confine myself to one, but one very significant, example. It concerns the American automobile industry, which has been greatly humbled in the last few years, despite all of the subsidies, counted in many billions of U.S. dollars, received from the world's most powerful capitalist state.

Let me quote from an article on the Ford corporation and its globalizing fantasies published way back in 1994 in *The Sunday Times*:

> Full globalization is being attempted by multinationals.... "This is definitely Trotman's baby," said one American source. "He has a vision of the future which says that, to be a global winner, Ford must be a truly global corporation." According to Trotman, who told *The Sunday Times* in October 1993, "As automotive competition becomes more global as we get into the next century, the pressure to find *scale economies* will become greater and greater. If, instead of making two engines of 500,000 units each, you can make 1 million units, then the costs are much lower. Ultimately there will be a handful of global players and the rest will either not be there or they will be struggling along." Trotman and his colleagues concluded that full globalization is the way to beat competitors such as the Japanese and, in Europe, Ford's archrival General Motors, which retains a cost-advantage over Ford. Ford also believes it needs globalization to capitalise on fast-emerging markets in the Far East and in Latin America.[9]

Thus, the only thing Alex Trotman—the British-born Chairman of Ford at the time—forgot to consider, despite his impeccable arithmetical skill of knowing the difference between 500,000 and one million, was this: what happens when they cannot sell the one million (and many times more) motor cars, despite the company's strategically envisaged and enjoyed cost-advantage. In the case of Ford, even the massive differential rate of exploitation which the company could impose worldwide as a huge transnational company—that is, paying the workers of Ford Philippines, for instance, one twenty-fifth what the company pays its workforce in the United States—is insufficient for securing a way out of this fundamental contradiction.

This is where we stand today, not only in the case of the badly humbled Ford but also in that of General Motors, irrespective of its cost-advantage, once deeply envied even by Ford.

Talking about a recently instituted deal, which provides major subsidies by the American state to the country's giant car companies, this is how the current situation of the U.S. automotive industry is described by *The Economist*: "The deal means that car companies—blessed with the government guarantee—should get loans with an interest rate of around 5% rather than [the]15% they would face on the open market in today's conditions."[10]

However, no subsidy of any kind can be considered satisfactory because the Big Three companies—General Motors, Ford, and Chrysler—are all on the brink of bankruptcy. Thus, *The Economist* must admit that:

> Once industrial subsidies like this begin to flow, it is difficult to stop them. A recent study by the Cato Institute, a rightwing think-tank, found that the federal government spent some $92 billion subsidising business in 2006 alone. Only $21 billion of that went to farmers: much of the rest went to firms such as Boeing, IBM, and General Electric in the form of export-credit support and various research subsidies. The Big Three are already complaining that it will take too long to dish out the [state] money, and they want the process speeded up. They also want a further $25 billion, possibly attached to the second version of the Wall Street rescue bill. The logic of bailing out Wall Street is that finance underpins everything. Detroit cannot begin to make that claim. But, given its successful lobbying, can it be long before ailing airlines and failing retailers join the queue?[11]

Financial adventurism, in the form of the immense expansion of speculative activities witnessed in the last three or four decades, is of course inseparable from the deepening crisis of the productive branches of industry and the ensuing trouble arising from utterly sluggish capital accumulation (and indeed failed accumulation). Now, inevitably, in the domain of industrial production the crisis is also getting much worse.

Naturally, the necessary consequence of the ever-deepening crisis in the productive branches of industry or the "real economy," as it is has come to be called, is the growth of unemployment everywhere on a fright-ening scale and the human misery associated with it. To expect a happy solution to these problems from the capitalist state's rescue operations would be a great illusion.

This is the context where our politicians should really begin to pay attention to the important lessons of history, instead of dishing out large dollops of public money. For as a result of historical development under the rule of capital in its structural crisis, in our own time we have reached the point where we must be subjected to the destructive impact of an ever worsening *symbiosis* between the state legislative framework of our socie-ty and the material productive as well as the financial dimension of the established societal reproductive order.

Understandably, that symbiotic relationship can be, and frequently it also happens to be, managed with utterly corrupt practices by the privi-leged personifications of capital, in business as much as in politics. For, no matter how corrupt such practices might be, they are fully in tune with the *institutionalized counter-values* of the established order. And—within the framework of the symbiosis prevailing between the economic field and the dominant political practices—they are legally quite permissible, thanks to the most dubious and often even clearly anti-democratic facili-tating role of the *impenetrable legislative jungle* provided in this respect by the state also in the financial domain.

Fraudulence, in a great variety of its practicable forms, is the *nor-mality of capital.* Its extremely destructive manifestations are by no means confined to the operation of the military-industrial complex. By now the direct role of the capitalist state in the parasitic world of finance is not only fundamentally important, in view of its all-pervasive magni-tude, as we found out with shocking clarity during the last few weeks, but also potentially catastrophic.

The embarrassing fact of the matter is that the giant U.S. mortgage companies, like Fannie Mae and Freddie Mac, were corruptly supported and generously supplied with highly profitable but totally undeserved guarantees by the American state's *legislative jungle* in the first place, as well as through the personal services of unpunished political corruption. Indeed, the capitalist state's ever-more dense legislative jungle happens to be the "democratic" legitimator of *institutionalized fraudulence* in our societies. The editors and journalists of *The Economist* are in fact perfectly well acquainted with the corrupt practices that, and here I quote their London-based weekly:

> allowed Fannie and Freddie to operate with *tiny amounts of capital*. The two groups had core capital (as defined by their regulator) of $83.2 billion at the end of 2007; this supported *$5.2 trillion* of debt and guarantees, *a gearing ratio of 65 to one*. [!!!] According to CreditSights, a research group, Fannie and Freddie were counterparties in *$2.3 trillion-worth* of derivative transactions, related to their *hedging activities*. There is no way a private bank would be allowed to have such a highly geared balance sheet,[12] nor would it *qualify for the highest AAA credit rating.*.... They used their *cheap financing* to buy *higher-yielding assets*."[13]
>
> Moreover, "with so much at stake, no wonder the companies built a formidable lobbying machine. *Ex-politicians were given jobs*. Critics could expect a rough ride. The companies were not afraid to bite the hands that fed them.[emphases added]"[14]

Not being afraid to bite the hands that fed them refers, of course, to the American state legislative body. But why should they be afraid? For such giant companies constitute a *total symbiosis* with the capitalist state. This corrupt relationship also asserts itself in terms of the personnel involved—through the act of hiring politicians who could serve them preferentially with a mind-boggling "gearing ratio of 65 to one" and the associated AAA credit rating.

4. U.S. DEFAULT IS BY NO
MEANS "UNTHINKABLE"

The gravity of the present situation is underlined in a characteristic way by the circumstance, reported in these words by *The Economist*: "traders in the credit-default swaps market have recently made *bets on the unthinkable: that America may default on its debt*."[15] Naturally, such traders react, even to events of such character and gravity, the only possible way they can: by squeezing profit out of them.

The big trouble for the global capital system is, though, that the *default of America is not unthinkable at all*. On the contrary, it is—and it has been for a very long time—a coming certainty. This is why I wrote many years ago that:

> In a world of financial *insecurity* nothing suits better the practice of gambling with astronomical and criminally unsecured sums on the world's stock exchanges—foreshadowing an earthquake of magnitude 9 or 10 on the financial "Richter scale"—than to call the enterprises which engage in such gambling "*securities* management".... When exactly and in what form—of which there can be several, more or less brutal, varieties—the U.S. will default on its astronomical debt, cannot be seen at this point in time. There can be only two certainties in this regard. The first is that the *inevitability of the American default* will deeply affect everyone on this planet. And the second, that the preponderant hegemonic power position of the U.S. will continue to be asserted in every way, so as to make the rest of the world pay for the American debt for as long as it is capable of doing.[16]

Of course, the aggravating condition today is that the rest of the world—even with the massive Chinese contribution to the balance sheet of the American Treasury—is less and less capable of filling the "black hole" produced on an ever-growing scale by America's insatiable appetite for debt financing, as demonstrated by the global reverberations of the recent U.S. mortgage and bank crisis. This circumstance brings the necessary default of America, in one of its more or less brutal varieties, that much nearer.

The truth of this disturbing matter is that there can be no way out of these ultimately suicidal contradictions—which are inseparable from the *imperative of endless capital-expansion, irrespective of the consequences*—without radically changing our mode of social metabolic reproduction. This demands adopting the responsible and rational practices of the only viable economy—an economy oriented by human need, instead of alienating, dehumanizing, and degrading profit.[17]

This is where the overwhelming impediment of capital's self-serving interdeterminations must be confronted, no matter how difficult it must be under the prevailing conditions. For the absolutely necessary adoption and the appropriate future development of the only viable economy is inconceivable without the radical transformation of the established socioeconomic and political order itself.

Gordon Brown recently voiced his displeasure with "unfettered capitalism," in the name of totally unspecified "regulation." You may remember that Gorbachev, too, wanted a kind of regulated capitalism, under the name of "market socialism," and you may also know what happened to him and to his grotesque daydream. On the other hand, British Conservative Prime Minister Edward Heath's expression, a very long time ago, for the same sin of unfettered capitalism was "the unacceptable face of capitalism." And yet, unfettered capitalism, despite its unacceptable face, remained all these decades not only acceptable but—in the course of its further development—it had become much worse. For the causal foundation of our ever-more serious problems is not the unacceptable face of unregulated capitalism but its *destructive substance.* It is that overpowering substance that *must resist and nullify* all efforts aimed at restraining the capital system even minimally—as, indeed, it actually succeeded in doing by metamorphosing (social democratic) Old Labour in Britain into (neoliberal) New Labour. Accordingly, the periodically renewed fantasy of *regulating capitalism* in a structurally significant way can only amount to trying to tie the wind into a knot.

Today, we have to face the gravity of capital's *structural crisis,* which calls for the institution of radical *systemic change.* No less a figure than the Deputy Governor of the Bank of England has described the current crisis as the greatest economic crisis in all of human history. It is most revealing about the incorrigible character of the capital system that even at a time like this, when the immense magnitude of the unfolding crisis cannot be denied any longer even by the system's most devoted *ex officio* apologists, nothing can be contemplated, not to mention actually done, for changing the fundamental defects of an ever more destructive societal reproductive order by those who control the economic and political levers of our society.

In contrast to the recent illumination by his own Deputy, the Governor of the Bank of England, Mervyn King, had no reservations at all about the soundness of the cherished capital system, nor did he have the faintest anticipation of a coming crisis, when he praised to the sky Martin Wolf's capital-apologetic book, with its self-complacent and peremptorily assertive title: *Why Globalization Works.* He called that book "a devastating intellectual critique of the opponents of globalization" and a "civilized, wise, and optimistic view of our economic and political future."[18] Now, however, everybody is forced to have at least some concern about the real nature and the necessary destructive consequences of dogmatically hailed *capitalist* globalization.

Naturally, my own attitude to Wolf's book was very different from that of Mervyn King and others who share the same vested interests. I commented at the time of its publication in 2004 that:

> the author, who is the Chief Economics Commentator of the London *Financial Times*, forgets to ask the really important question: *For whom does it work?*, if it does. It certainly works, for the time being, and by no means that well, for the decision-makers of transnational capital, but not for the overwhelming majority of humankind who must suffer the consequences. And no amount of *"jurisdictional integration"* advocated by the author—that is, in plain English, the tighter direct control of the deplored "too many states" by a handful of imperialist powers, especially the biggest one of them—is going to remedy the situation. Capitalist globalization in reality does not work and cannot work. For it cannot overcome the irreconcilable contradictions and antagonisms manifest through the global structural crisis of the system. Capitalist globalization itself is the contradictory manifestation of that crisis, trying to overturn the *cause/effect* relationship in a vain attempt to cure some negative effects by other *wishfully projected effects*, because it is structurally incapable of addressing their *causes*.[19]

In this sense, recent attempts to counter the intensifying symptoms of the crisis by the cynically camouflaged nationalization of astronomic magnitudes of capitalist bankruptcy, out of yet to be invented state resources, only highlight the deep-seated and antagonistic causal determinations of the capital system's destructiveness. For what is fundamentally at stake today is not simply a massive financial crisis but humanity's potential self-destruction at this juncture of historical development, through both military conflagration and the ongoing destruction of nature.

Despite the concerted manipulation of interest rates and the vacuous summit meetings of the dominant capitalist countries, nothing has been lastingly achieved by throwing gobs of money into the bottomless hole of the "crunched" global financial market. The *comprehensive global answer to the confidence gap*, as wishfully projected by *The Economist* and its masters, belongs to the world of fantasy. For one of the greatest historic failures of capital, as the long-established mode of social metabolic control, is the continued dominance of the potentially most aggressive *nation states* and the impossibility of instituting *the state of the capital system as such* on the basis of the structurally entrenched antagonisms of this system.

To imagine that within the framework of such antagonistic causal determinations a harmonious permanent solution could be found to the deepening structural crisis of a most iniquitous production and exchange order—which is now actively engaged in producing a global food crisis on top of all of its other crying contradictions, including the ever more pervasive destruction of nature—is the worst kind of wishful thinking, bordering on total irrationality. And the so-called jurisdictional integration of the too many states under a self-appointed few, or one, as advocated by some prominent capital-apologists, can only suggest the permanence of potentially suicidal global imperialist domination.

This is why Marx is more relevant today than ever before. For only a radical *systemic change* can offer historically sustainable hope and a solution for the future.

CHAPTER TWO

The Present Crisis[1]

1. SURPRISING ADMISSIONS

As a point of departure, let us explore three rather surprising statements made by some well-known British public figures. The first asserted that:

> We are on the brink of economic crisis—a crisis with social and political consequences we have barely begun to contemplate. [We are facing] continuing decline—and in its wake social and political decay and perhaps even democracy itself struggling for survival.[2]

The second warned that the immense amount of money which the United States annually spent on defense "created major problems," adding that:

> It is spent largely within one market, which is perhaps the most protected market in the alliance—by technology transfer regulations, by American protection laws, by extraterritorial controls . . . co-ordinated through the Pentagon and protected by Congress. It is channelled into the largest and richest companies on earth. It is irresistible and if unchecked it will . . . buy its way through sector after sector of the world's advanced technologies. . . . The way

in which the reconstruction of the Westland PLC [a British aircraft company] has been handled has raised profound issues about defence procurement and Britain's future as a technologically advanced country.[3]

The third statement was no less dramatic. With reference to President Reagan's so-called Strategic Defense Initiative (SDI), it protested against the negative implications of SDI for British industry, declaring that:

> We are being tempted by crumbs from the table. Europe should be careful that participation in the U.S. Star Wars research programme will not amount to taking in a Trojan horse.[4]

What is surprising in all of this is not that such statements have been made at all, but the social and political allegiances of the people who made them. For the first warning came from Sir Edwin Nixon, Chairman of IBM in the United Kingdom. Nor was the second admonition voiced by a flaming revolutionary or even by someone committed to the cause of the soft left. On the contrary, it was made by none other than the Tory Party's former Secretary of State for Defence in Britain, Michael Heseltine, in an attempt to explain why he had to resign and create a major political scandal on account of the government's pretended neutrality (and actual support) for the American transnational corporations against the European Consortium. And finally, the third statement came from Paddy Ashdown, Liberal Party Member of Parliament for Yeovil. The same man who vociferously defended the successful American takeover bid for the Westland helicopter company, which Heseltine protested.

The point is that capitalism today is experiencing a profound crisis that can no longer be denied even by its spokesmen and beneficiaries. Nor should one imagine that U.S. capital is less affected by it than British and European capital. IBM's Vice Chairman for research asserted recently, with a heavy touch of irony, that the much prophesied "*technological spin-off*"—in the name of which prohibitively expensive and corruptly overcharged defense contracts have been enthusiastically advocated by many and approved by Parliaments and governments in the past— turned out to be no more than a mere "*drip-off*."[5] Indeed, the overall situation is in reality much more serious than the non-materialization of the promised technological side benefits of military waste could suggest on its own.[6]

Instead of the promised commercial bonanza, a significant worsening of competitiveness resulted from the military-orientated distortion of capitalist cost-accounting both in Europe and in the United States. For "as military technology has become more and more complex, expensive, clever, and arcane, it has increasingly diverged from possible civilian applications."[7]

Accordingly, among the major disadvantages underlined by a report on information technology research and development (issued by the U.S. Congress Office of Technology Assessment) we find: "security classifications which tend to slow advancement in technology; rigid technical specifications for military procurement which have limited utility for commercial applications; and the 'consumption' of limited, valuable scientific and engineering resources for military purposes, which may inhibit commercial developments."[8]

In other words, direct state intervention in the capitalist reproduction process ultimately misfires, constraining the course of civilian economic development (and by no means only with its secretive political and administrative rules). Also, it produces major problems in tangible economic terms by generating absurd technical specifications (e.g., the nuclear-blast-proof toilet seat that survives the incineration of its occupier) and the commercially useless productive and engineering practices corresponding to them. At the same time, moreover, we are also confronted with the extreme *technologization of science* that straitjackets its productive potentialities even in strictly capitalist consumer-economic terms, in the service of utterly wasteful military purposes.

2. THE ASSERTION OF U.S. HEGEMONY

The negative consequences of such declining competitiveness are unavoidable. They are already noticeable in the intensification of the contradictions of international trade relations and in the measures adopted by the most powerful capitalist country to reassert in an openly aggressive fashion the long unchallenged U.S. dominance within the Western alliance. Let us consider some instances of major importance.

2.1 "Extra-Territoriality"

This issue came to light in parliamentary debates during the summer of 1985. Since it negatively affected various sections of British capital, it could be taken up by all shades of opinion in the parliamentary spectrum.

Liberal MP Paddy Ashdown claimed that: "U.S. attempts to control the export of high technology systems could destroy the U.K. computer industry." He also claimed that the U.S. Export of Goods Control Order would introduce "a series of potentially fatal export constraints, imposed at the behest of the Pentagon and without adequate consultation with any of the industries affected in the U.K." Furthermore, Ashdown asserted that the United States was turning the law in question to its commercial gain, to quash competition from U.K. companies, alleging that 500,000 jobs already have been lost in Europe as a result.

In reply to Ashdown's representations, the Conservative British Attorney General, Sir Michael Havers, described the U.S. control attempts as an "unwarranted encroachment of U.K. jurisdiction and *contrary to international law*."[9] Ironically, however, by the beginning of 1987 the British Government had capitulated on the issue in a humiliating way, accepting the earlier rhetorically condemned unwarranted encroachment on U.K. jurisdiction. It conferred on U.S. trade inspectors the right to examine the books of British manufacturing companies that use American high technology components, despite the protests of U.K. firms, which fear that information thus obtained from their company records could damage them.

Plessey's director of strategic planning, John Saunders, commented that the company's books contained information that could be useful to U.S. competitors. At the same time, Liberal MP Michael Meadowcroft protested that U.K. sovereignty was breached by the move. "It is a *monstrous interference*," he said.[10]

Naturally, the Labour Party had also joined in the debates. Labour MP Michael Meacher claimed that the Government sacrificed U.K. interests "in its total failure to protect British companies who find themselves the prey of unfair American domination and interference." He also suggested that the issue of sovereignty should be a key issue in the 1987 general election.[11]

2.2 Industrial Advantage from Military Secrecy

Two issues stand out in this respect. The first, under the organization of the Coordianting Committee on Multilateral Export controls (COCOM)—masterminded by Pentagon hawk Richard Perle—is concerned with the imposition of severe export restrictions on Western European countries, to the clear advantage of U.S. firms.

The second was highlighted in connection with Reagan's Strategic Defense Initiative (SDI). Many British scientists and computer experts protested against the whole initiative and the way in which it was handled by the government. Richard Ennals of Imperial College, the former research director of the Alvey project, was the first U.K. scientist to resign over the issue. He commented forcefully: "SDI is sucking in British technology for U.S. industrial exploitation."[12] Thus, it came as no great surprise that his book—in which he developed his criticisms at length—was suppressed a few days before its publication by his own publishers. (One can quite easily guess the quarters from which the pressure for suppressing his book had come.)

Moreover, the attitude to SDI was a matter of serious concern even in some European governmental circles. It has been reported that:

> The European Commission is warning Common Market governments that European participation in the American Star Wars programme could damage the health of pan-European research programmes like Esprit and domestic projects like Alvey. The commission has sent a confidential letter to the 10 member governments ahead of the Common Market summit in Milan later this month, warning that participation in the space defence initiative can be very damaging to high-technology industry. The letter warns that European participation in Star Wars research would divert European research efforts. Apart from threatening Alvey and Esprit, it would seriously diminish overall European research [and] then boost the constraints which are already being unilaterally imposed by the United States on European hi-tech trade.[13]

Irrespective of what might or might not be done eventually about such concerns by the particular European governments, it is impossible to ignore the severity of the underlying contradictions.

2.3 Direct Trade Pressures Applied by the U.S. Legislative and Executive

Some recent examples include the *agricultural tariffs war* threatened by the Reagan Administration—over which the governments of the European Economic Community in the end capitulated—and the European Air Bus project over which they have refused to capitulate so far. Conflict with Japan also intensifies, as recently underlined by the unanimous vote of the U.S. Senate in favor of strong protectionist measures against Japan and duly followed by the application of some punitive tariffs.

But well beyond such particular confrontations, there is the prospect of abandoning altogether the framework of the General Agreement on Tariffs and Trade (GATT) as the institutional regulator of tariff agreements between the U.S. and Europe. We can now witness, in the United States, a growing pressure to switch from such *multilateral* regulators of commercial interchange to strictly bilateral trade agreements through which the incomparably more powerful American side could dictate conditions to much smaller and weaker European competitors, taken separately. For bilateral trade relations—by their very nature—always favor the stronger party involved in such contracts, enhancing its relative advantage in more ways than one.

Whether or not the growing pressures for undermining or leaving GATT—as well as similar moves directed at other mechanisms of regulation—will prevail is, at this point, an open question. What is, nevertheless, highly significant is that the need for a drastic restructuring of American trade relations with the rest of the world on a *bilateral* basis is being seriously contemplated at all.

2.4 The Real Debt Problem

There is a great deal of discussion concerning the severe and by now obviously unmanageable indebtedness of Latin American countries, as well as the dangerous implications of such indebtedness for the world financial system as a whole. While no one should wish to deny the importance of this issue, it must be stressed that it is quite astonishing how little attention is paid to the need to put it in perspective. For the entire Latin American debt, amounting to less than $350 billion at the time of writing this article (which had been collectively accumulated by the countries concerned over a period of several decades) pales into total insignificance if set against U.S. indebtedness, both internal and external, which must be counted in *trillions* of dollars; i.e., in magnitudes that quite simply defy the imagination.

Characteristically, however, this matter is kept out of sight most of the time, thanks to the conspiracy of silence of the interested parties. It is as if such astronomical debts could be "written into the chimney breast, so as to let the soot take care of them," to borrow a Hungarian adage (about small debts incurred among close friends who can easily cope with such "write-offs"). Yet, to imagine that this practice of debt-management, involving trillions of dollars, could go on indefinitely strains the limits of all credulity.

Admittedly, the partners to such practices—the European countries no less than Japan—are locked into a system of heavy dependency on U.S. markets and on the concomitant debt-generated "liquidity." Thus, they are in a very precarious position when it comes to devising effective measures for bringing under control the real debt problem. Indeed, they are sucked deeper and deeper into the whirlpool of those contradictory determinations whereby they "voluntarily" increase their own dependence on the escalating American debt, with all of its dangers, while helping to promote and finance it.

From the fact that this vicious circle exists, it does not follow that the global capitalist system can escape the perilous implications of trillions of American dollars mounting on the wrong side of the balance sheet. In fact, the limits of how long such practices can be maintained should not be too difficult to identify.

To be sure, the Western capitalist countries—partly due to the internal contradictions of their own economies and partly because of their heavy dependence on American commodity and financial markets—will continue to participate with their financial assets in safeguarding the relative stability of the U.S. economy and, thereby, of the global system. For the adventurist dominance of *finance capital* is, in general, the *manifestation* of deep-seated economic crises rather than their *cause,* even if, in its turn, it greatly contributes to their subsequent aggravation. Thus, the tendency to destroy certain industries and to transfer much of the financial assets thereby generated to the United States is by no means accidental. (Though, of course, it is utterly grotesque that Britain, for instance, which leads the capitalist world in the process of "deindustrialization," should also be one of the principal *creditor* countries today.) Nor should it be surprising that once the assets of a country are deployed in this way, the pressure for protecting them against the danger of a disastrous financial chain-reaction and ultimate collapse—by transferring further funds, supporting the dollar through the manipulative intervention of central banks, and so forth—becomes quite irresistible.

Nevertheless, only fools and blind apologists could deny that the ongoing U.S. practice of debt management is built on very shaky ground. It will become totally untenable when the rest of the world (including the "Third World" from which massive transfers are still successfully extracted in one way or another every year) is no longer in a position to *produce* the resources that the American economy requires in order to maintain itself in existence as the idealized engine of the capitalist world economy.

2.5 Political Antagonism Arising from U.S. Economic Penetration

In the midst of a recent political scandal, following the exposure of secret government negotiations with giant U.S. firms, the leader of the British Labour Party talked of "a *further act of colonization* in the British economy."[14] He received the full approval of the liberal press. An editorial in *The Guardian* protested:

> First there was United Technologies, negotiating to take a stake in Westland [and succeeding, through governmental manipulation and suspect share dealings, under the cloak of secrecy]. Then General Motors with Lotus; then a threat to take the contract for airborne radar away from GEC [which, also,

later turned into an accomplished fact] and lob it into the hands of Boeing. Now, Ford may buy BL, all that remains of a British-owned motor industry. One or two of these deals might have been excusable. But so many, so close, give the impression that Mrs. Thatcher has such little faith in U.K. manufacturers that she wants to turn the country into a *Third World assembler of multinational products*.[15]

Ironically, it was not the Labour leadership but the same editorial article in *The Guardian* that pointed out the grave implications of such economic takeovers for the position of labor. It reminded its readers of the direct threat of increasing unemployment as a matter of transnational industrial policy—cynically spelled out by the management of one of the principal U.S. companies—and also added to its critical concern a warning about the consequences of American penetration into the British economy for the balance of payments and for the future of British industry in general:

> Mr Bob Lutz, chairman of Ford of Europe, recently told the *Financial Times*: "If we find we have major assembly facilities regardless of the country involved, which for one reason or another—perhaps *uneducated government* action (giving *longer holidays,* a *shorter working week*) or *union intransigence*—cannot be competitive, we *would not shy away from a decision to close them*."
>
> Ford U.K. . . . is also a substantial drain on the balance of payments, amounting to £1.3 billion in 1983 as it (quite properly from its own self-interest) sourced from the cheaper imports.
>
> The Government claims not to have an industrial strategy. In fact, of course, it has one. Privatise everything that moves and sell what you can to foreign buyers. You don't have to be a *Little Englander* to realise that this is an abdication of responsibility which could make the *terminal decline of industry* in this country a self-fulfilling prophecy.[16]

But, of course, the heaviest irony arises from the peculiar circumstance that all of this is happening against the background of massive American indebtedness.

Senator McGovern, at the time of his Presidential campaign, pointed out that the United States was running the Vietnam War on credit cards. Since then, U.S. capital has graduated to pursue much bigger stakes in financial terms. Its deep penetration not only into the "Third World" but also into the heartlands of "advanced capitalism," through the relentless pursuit of its *credit card imperialism,* points to a major contradiction that cannot be hidden away indefinitely even by the most servile of "friendly governments" (like Mrs. Thatcher's Conservative one), as the growing number of protests coming from the adversely affected capitalist circles testify.

The most important, and potentially most harmful, dimension of this economic penetration is that it is being pursued—with the full complicity of the most powerful sections of capital in the Western countries concerned—on the basis of an already astronomical, and inexorably growing, U.S. indebtedness that foreshadows an *ultimate default* of quite unimaginable magnitude.

But even with regard to the modality of the financial operations involved, it is rather revealing that the major U.S. takeovers of foreign companies are often financed from credit raised internally, in the affected countries themselves, diverting much needed resources to *financing American credit card imperialism.*

Furthermore, there is frequently also a direct connection with the interests of the military-industrial complex and the lucrative military contracts, often constituting the hidden motivation behind takeover deals, which happen to be vital to maintaining the profitability of the dominant capitalist corporations.

A characteristic example came to light in the debates over the secret deal between the British Government and General Motors—foiled as a result of the political scandal that followed its revelation—concerning British Leyland's truck division as well as Land Rover. In the parliamentary debate over this affair:

> Alan Williams MP, a Labour industry spokesman, said that the defence implications of a U.S. takeover of Land Rover had not been considered. A subsidiary of Land Rover called Self-Change Gear supplied components to the British-made battle tank and was in contention for a *£200 million contract* for the American battle tank. Its major competitor was General Motors, to whom the Government was now considering selling it.[17]

Here, the issue was that had the secret deal been materialized—that is, had it been simply presented to Parliament and to the public by the British Government, at an opportune moment, as an accomplished fact to which "There is no alternative,"—General Motors not only would have acquired, *for absolutely nothing,* British Leyland's truck division as well as, and more importantly, its Land Rover division but at the same time it would have also pocketed a very handsome profit on top of its free acquisitions, as a side benefit.

Such practices, however, can only generate conflicts, even in formerly unsuspected quarters, and intensify the pressure for protectionist measures. A pressure which not so long ago—at the time of the postwar expansionary phase of capitalist development and its concomitant consensus—could be safely ignored in view of its limited extent and subterranean character. Ominously, however, under the present conjuncture the protectionist pressure tends to erupt into the open in all of the important areas of global capitalist economic and interstate relations, aggravating thereby the various contradictions of the system on which it has a direct or indirect bearing.

3. WISHFUL THINKING ABOUT THE DECLINE OF THE U.S. AS A HEGEMONIC POWER

It might be tempting to overstate the gravity and immediacy of the present crisis. This, however, risks jumping to the kind of conclusion we were offered five years ago in a book co-authored by four highly respected left-wing intellectuals who prematurely announced "the decline of the United States as a hegemonic power."[18]

Such a view directly contradicts Paul Baran's characterization of the radically altered postwar international power relationships in the capitalist world. He described "the unabated rivalry among the imperialist countries as well as the growing inability of the old imperialist nations to hold their own in face of the American quest for expanded influence and power,"[19] insisting that "the assertion of American supremacy in the 'free' world implies the reduction of Britain and France (not to speak of Belgium, Holland, and Portugal) to the status of junior partners of American imperialism."[20]

Baran's diagnosis, made more than three decades ago, has stood the test of time. In fact, there is as of yet no serious sign of the wishfully anticipated decline of the United States as a hegemonic power, notwithstanding the appearance of numerous symptoms of crisis in the global system. For the contradictions that we can identify concern the whole of the interlocking system of global capital in which American capital occupies, maintains, and indeed continues to strengthen its dominant position in every way, paradoxically even through its—on the face of it quite vulnerable, yet up to the present time successfully enforced—practice of credit card imperialism.

People who speak of, and attach so much significance to, the alleged decline of the U.S. as a hegemonic power seem to forget that such possibilities—i.e., the many ways of imposing astronomical U.S. indebtedness on the rest of the world and disregarding its unavoidable negative implications for the other capitalistically advanced societies—are available only to one single country, in virtue of its practically undisputed (and, short of a major socioeconomic earthquake, undisputable) hegemonic power within the capitalist world.

One set of rules of good housekeeping is reserved for one single member of the club of advanced capitalism, and a very different set is imposed on all the others, including Japan and West Germany. What is that if not evidence for the continued hegemonic supremacy of the United States? Besides, even on the terrain of *ideology*, we can observe in the postwar period, and particularly in the last decade, a remarkable *strengthening* of American hegemony, rather than its weakening, as postulated by the end of U.S. hegemony thesis. This ideological domination is—to a far from negligible extent—materially sustained by the credit-card-financed "brain drain" in which European "jet-set-socialist intellectuals" participate on a permanent or part-time basis (no less than their natural science research colleagues in the domain of technology). And the fact that, as a feedback from such participation, they actively help to diffuse on this side of the Atlantic, not only in academic circles but also among the leadership of Western working-class parties and trade unions, the dominant American liberal discourse on so-called feasible socialism, only underlines the sobering truth that economic supremacy can produce most unexpected forms of ideological mystification.

4. THE OFFICIAL VIEW OF HEALTHY EXPANSION

All the same, it hardly can be denied that something significantly new is happening to the system as a whole. Its nature cannot be explained, as is often attempted, simply in terms of a traditional *cyclic crisis,* since both the *scope* and the *duration* of the crisis, which we have been subjected to in the last two decades, has well overreached the historically known limits of cyclic crises. Nor is it really plausible to ascribe the identifiable crisis symptoms to the so-called *long wave*: an idea which, as a somewhat mysterious explanatory hypothesis, has been naïvely or apologetically injected into more recent debates.

As the crisis symptoms multiply and their severity is aggravated, it looks much more likely that the system as a whole is approaching certain *structural limits* of capital, even though it would be far too optimistic to suggest that the capitalist mode of production has already reached the point of no return leading to its collapse. Nevertheless, we must face up to the prospect of very serious complications when the U.S. debt default reverberates over the global economy with all its might in the not too distant future. After all, we should not forget that the U.S. Government has defaulted already—under Richard Nixon's Presidency—on its solemn pledge concerning the gold convertibility of the dollar, without the slightest regard for the interests of those directly affected by its decision, and indeed without any concern whatsoever for the severe implications of its unilateral action for the future of the international monetary system.

Recently, we came a considerable step nearer to the U.S. debt default with the record April–June 1987 trade deficit, amounting to $39.53 billion, of which $15.71 billion represented the month of June alone: yet another all-time record. For even the April–June figure (constituting an annual sum of nearly $160 billion) well exceeds the *total* accumulated debt of Argentina and Brazil put together; not to speak of the annual $188.52 billion trade deficit which we are heading for on the basis of the June 1987 figure. At the same time, as if he wanted to underline the total unreality of the adopted remedial measures:

Mr Robert Heller, Federal Reserve Governor, said yesterday that the U.S. economy was becoming more balanced, noting that "what we are seeing is a healthy continuation of the current economic expansion."[21]

If $188.52 billion annual balance of trade deficit, coupled with astronomical budgetary deficits, can be considered the healthy continuation of economic expansion, one shudders to think what the *unhealthy* condition of the economy will look like when we reach it.

5. POSTSCRIPT 1995: THE MEANING OF "BLACK MONDAYS" (AND WEDNESDAYS)

A few weeks after the completion of this article—to be precise: on Monday, October 19, 1987—we witnessed the spectacle of a big tumble on the world's stock exchanges. This must have been still part of the healthy continuation of economic expansion, since it happened so soon after the reassuring statement made by the U.S. Federal Reserve Governor. The aftermath of this event was also very interesting and, to the world of big business, no doubt also reassuring. For the governments of the capitalistically advanced countries instituted some binding regulations and corresponding computer mechanisms, with a view to calling a temporary halt to all stock market activity in the event of "excessive speculative transactions," in order to prevent a repetition of "Black Monday," as October 19, 1987 came to be known.

Strangely, however, all this had very little effect on the events leading to "Black Wednesday" in 1992, and the (purported) "forced abandonment" of the European Exchange Rate Mechanism by the British Government. For the Bank of England always had the resources to eat speculative Fund Managers, like George Soros, for breakfast by the dozen; on this occasion, however, it was decided, instead, to reward his enterprise with $1 billion in exchange for the convenient excuse that Britain was "forced out" of the European system of monetary regulation and, therefore, could not help breaking its treaty obligations. Naturally, the result of this move was an almost 30 percent devaluation of the pound sterling and with it the acquisition of a significant competitive advantage against the country's European partners—precisely what the Exchange Rate Mechanism was designed to prevent—and an "export-led recovery," which has been hailed ever since by the British government. The greatly devalued currency's competitive advantage helps a great deal—even if by no means forever—in the field of exports, although it refuses to deliver the frequently announced "full recovery" and "healthy expansion" for the economy as a whole.

Three years before Black Monday, the sorrowful but, for the financial world, happy-ending tale of Black Sunday had hit the headlines. At that time:

> The Bank of England was called into action to save an important institution when Johnson Matthey Bankers (JMB), the bullion trader, collapsed and had to be rescued by a Bank-organized lifeboat. That crisis broke on a Sunday and after holding a council of war with City elders, the Bank took JMB into *public ownership*.[22]

The disastrous collapse of Barings Securities—one of the oldest banking institutions in Britain, founded in 1772, and once described as the sixth great power of Europe, after Britain, France, Austria, Russia, and Prussia—unfolded in February 1995 on a *Black Saturday*, followed by another *Black Sunday*:

> The crisis stunned senior City figures. Sir Michael Richardson, one of the Square Mile's [the London City's] most respected bankers, said last night: "This is the most devastating news, and one of the most serious things I have heard in ages."[23]

Barings, alas, could not be rescued. The customary way of dealing with large-scale failures—by taking the enterprises concerned into "public ownership" (so much despised by the champions of "privatization" and market-idolatry) and, thereby, "nationalizing" private capitalist bankruptcy—cannot always do the trick, in the absence of a bottomless public purse. There was more than a touch of irony in the collapse of Barings, in that before its fate was sealed on the Singapore stock exchange "it had been weakened by heavy losses on its South American business, following the collapse of the Mexican peso."[24] Thus, what was supposed to be one of the great historical advances of present-day capitalism—modernizing globalization—had gone sour not only in Mexico, with the most painful consequences for its people. It contributed, at the same time, also to the ignominious liquidation of one of the most venerable and bluest of blue City institutions.

Black Tuesday by contrast, happened in the most unexpected place, even if it was fully in tune with the logic of capital. After only a few years of enjoying the blessings of "marketization" and monetary "convertibility," the Russian economy suffered a major shock—on Tuesday, October 11, 1994—through a catastrophic fall of the (already absurdly undervalued) ruble against the dollar. Thus, we are not only witnessing the same kind of crises erupt, with discomforting frequency, even in the once financially sheltered corners of the world, but also seem to be running out of days of the week to be blackened, as befits the system.

The day after *Black Monday*, a group of high-powered bankers and leading economists discussed the crisis on BBC television. One of them argued that the root cause of the disaster was the American debt and the failure to do something about it. Yet, the most cynical of the City bankers hit the nail on the head when he rebutted that the one thing much more disastrous than not doing anything about the American debt would be to attempt to do something about it.

It is only right and proper that an economic system riddled with contradictions should find its guiding principles in the topsy-turvy world of apologetic economic wisdom. In a world of utmost financial insecurity, nothing better suits the practice of gambling with astronomical and criminally unsecured sums on the world's stock exchanges—foreshadowing an earthquake of magnitude nine or ten on the financial "Richter scale"—than to call the enterprises that engage in such gambling "securities management"; a fact highlighted by the demise of "Barings Securities." In the same vein, one of the recent discoveries of "economic science" is called the "confidence coefficient," which is supposed to measure and depict on a "scientific graph"—on the basis of the most fanciful hearsay and wishful thinking—the health and future prospects of the capitalist economy. An even more recent rejoinder of equal explanatory value is the much talked about "feel-good factor," which is supposed to demonstrate that everything is all right with the economy, when to every sane person matters are visibly and painfully wrong. Some high-flown and respectably sounding economic categories fully match the apologetic intent.

Thus, the notions of "negative growth," meaning *recession*, and "sustained negative growth," equivalent to *depression*, mystify us. In accord with these concepts, even in dire trouble, there can be nothing to worry about. In the meantime, the Japanese Nikkei average, which fell from its peak of 40,000 to around the perilous 14,000 level at present—not in a single Black Day, but over five years of "sustained negative growth"—is very near to precipitating a global financial crisis. For below 14,000 "many of the shares held by Japan's banks and insurers will be worth less than the institutions paid for them."[25] And that is where yet another "economic category" is supposed to help. It is called "negative equity," which translates into human language as being in the immediate vicinity of bankruptcy.

Many millions of mortgage holders all over the world share the privilege of "negative equity" with Japan's banks and other economic institutions; but they are most unlikely to derive any reassurance from such an exalted financial status. For already hundreds of thousands of them have lost their homes, and many more are being *repossessed*—for which there seems to be no soothing category in contemporary "economic science"— and they refuse to "feel good" about it. As to Japan itself, the astronomical amount of "negative equity" possessed by its financial institutions has potentially disastrous economic consequences on account of the necessity to withdraw huge external capital funds, primarily from the Unites States. The repercussions of such a move would affect the whole of the global financial market.

The American hegemony discussed here was clamorously underlined also with the implosion of the Soviet system, and, even if far from uncontested, remains a major determining factor for world economic development in the foreseeable future.

When exactly and in what form—of which there can be several, more or less directly brutal, varieties—the United States will default on its astronomical debt, cannot be seen at this point in time. There can be only two certainties in this regard. The first is that the inevitability of the American default will deeply affect everyone on this planet. And the second, that the preponderant hegemonic power position of the United States will continue to be asserted in every way, so as to make the rest of the world pay for the American debt for as long as it is capable of doing so.

Two brief passages should illustrate the continued assertion of American hegemony. The first concerns the Newly Industrialized Countries (NICs):

> Not facing a debt crisis, the NICs have been able to avoid Structural Adjustment Programs [ruthlessly imposed on indebted "developing countries" by the United States]. They have not, however, been able to avoid the pressure of rollback. *Dark Victory*[26] shows how the U.S. government has repeatedly used the threat of trade war to force NIC states to reduce their economic activity and open up their economies to U.S. imports and investment. The new GATT agreement is an important part of the U.S. offensive. Although promoted as a generalized free trade agreement, it is primarily designed to restrict state direction of economic activity.[27]

The second quotation reminds us of the constant pressure applied by the United States, even on one of the economic giants of advanced capitalism, Germany, much the same way as on Japan. As we learn from an editorial article in *The Financial Times*:

> Calls from Washington for smaller fiscal deficits must be intensely irritating to the Germans. U.S. policymakers have, after all, called for a fiscal boost by Germany almost every year since the G7 was formed. More irritating still, the U.S. has itself followed the most consistently profligate fiscal policy of the three major economies. If global interest rates are to fall—as, indeed, they must—the U.S. must put its own fiscal house in order.[28]

However, there is a limit to everything, even to U.S. profligacy. The limit in this respect is that the average gross public debt of the OECD economies has grown in just two decades—between 1974 and 1994—from *35 percent* to *71 percent*. Given the same trend of development, it will not take many decades before it will be unavoidable to actually "do something" about these intractable problems, disregarding the views of City bankers and other vested interests.

CHAPTER THREE

The Necessity of Social Control[1]

In the deeply moving final pages of one of his last works Isaac Deutscher wrote:

> The technological basis of modern society, its structure and its conflicts are international or even universal in character; they tend towards international or universal solutions. And there are the unprecedented dangers threatening our biological existence. These, above all, press for the unification of mankind, which cannot be achieved without an integrating principle of social organization. . . . The present ideological deadlock and the social status quo hardly serve as the basis either for the solution of the problems of our epoch or even for mankind's survival. Of course, it would be the ultimate disaster if the nuclear superpowers were to treat the social status quo as their plaything and if either of them tried to alter it by force of arms. In this sense the peaceful co-existence of East and West is a paramount historic necessity. But the social status quo cannot be perpetuated. Karl Marx speaking about stalemates in past class struggles notes that they usually ended "in the common ruin of the contending classes." A stalemate indefinitely prolonged and guaranteed by a perpetual balance of nuclear deterrents, is sure to lead the contending classes and nations to their common and ultimate ruin. Humanity needs unity for its sheer survival; where can it find it if not in socialism.[2]

Deutscher concluded his work by passionately stressing: "*de nostra re agitur*"—it is all our own concern. Thus, it seems to me right to address ourselves on this occasion to some of the vital problems which stood at the centre of his interest towards the end of his life.

All the more so because the status quo in question is a historically unique status quo: one which inevitably involves the *whole* of mankind. As we all know from history, no status quo has ever lasted indefinitely; not even the most partial and localized ones. The permanence of a *global* status quo, with the immense and necessarily expanding dynamic forces involved in it, is a contradiction in terms: an absurdity which should be visible even to the most myopic of game theorists. In a world made up of a multiplicity of conflicting and mutually interacting social systems—in contrast to the fantasy world of escalating and deescalating chess boards—the precarious global status quo is *bound* to be broken for certain. The question is not "whether or not," but "by what means"? Will it be broken by devastating military means or will there be adequate social outlets for the manifestation of the rising social pressures which are in evidence today even in the most remote corners of our global social environment? The answer will depend on our success or failure in creating the necessary strategies, movements, and instruments capable of securing an effective transition towards a socialist society in which humanity can find the unity it needs for its sheer survival.

1. THE COUNTERFACTUAL CONDITIONALS OF APOLOGETIC IDEOLOGY

What we are experiencing today is not only a growing polarization—inherent in the global structural crisis of present-day capitalism—but, to multiply the dangers of explosion, also the breakdown of a whole series of safety valves, which played a vital part in the perpetuation of commodity society.

The change that undermined the power of consensus politics, the narrow institutionalization and integration of social protest, and the easy exportation of internal violence, through its transference to the plane of mystifying international collisions, has been quite dramatic. For not so

long ago the unhindered growth and multiplication of the power of capital, the irresistible extension of its rule over all aspects of human life, used
to be confidently preached and widely believed. The unproblematic and
undisturbed functioning of capitalist power structures was taken for
granted. It was declared to be a permanent feature of human life itself, and
the guardians of the hegemony of bourgeois culture dismissed those who
dared to doubt the wisdom of such declarations of faith as "hopeless ideologists."

But where now are the days when one of President Kennedy's principal theorists and advisers could speak about Marx and the social movements associated with his name in terms like these:

> He [Marx] applied his kit-bag to what he could perceive of one historical
> case: the case of the British take-off and drive to maturity. . . . Like the
> parochial intellectual of Western Europe he was, the prospects in Asia and
> Africa were mainly beyond his ken, dealt with almost wholly in the context of
> British policy rather than in terms of their own problems of *modernization.* . . .
> Marx created *a monstrous guide to public policy.* [Communism] is a kind of
> disease which can befall a transitional society if it fails to organize effectively
> those elements within it which are prepared to get on with the job of modern-
> ization. [In opposition to the Marxist approach the task is to create] in asso-
> ciation with the non-Communist politicians and peoples of the early take-off
> areas [i.e., the territories of neocolonialism] a partnership which will *see them
> through* into sustained growth on a political and social basis which keeps
> open the possibilities of progressive democratic development.[3]

These lines were written hardly a decade ago, but they read today like
prehistoric reasoning, although—or perhaps because—the author, Walt
Rostow, is a professor of economic history at the Massachusetts Institute
of Technology.

In this short decade, we were provided with tragically ample oppor-
tunity to see in practice, in Vietnam and in Cambodia, as well as in other
countries, the real meaning of the program of "partnership" intended "to
see the politicians of the early take-off areas through" to the disastrous
results of such partnership,[4] under the intellectual guidance of "brain
trusts" which included quite a few Walt Rostows: men who had the cyn-

ical insolence to call Marx's work "a monstrous guide to public policy." Inflated by the "arrogance of military power," they "proved," by means of tautologies interspersed with retrospective "deductions," that the American stage of economic growth is immune to all crisis.[5] They argued as well, with the help of counterfactual conditionals, that the break in the chain of imperialism was merely an unfortunate mishap, which, strictly speaking, should not have happened at all. For: *"if the First World War had not occurred, or had occurred a decade later, Russia would almost certainly have made a successful transition to modernization and rendered itself invulnerable to Communism."*[6]

We might be tempted to rejoice at the sight of such a level of intellectual power in our adversaries, were it not terrifying to contemplate the naked power they wield in virtue of their willing submission to the alienated institutions which demand "theories" of this kind, so as to follow, undisturbed even by the possibility of an occasional doubt, their blind collision course. The hollow constructions, which meet this demand of rationalization, are built on the pillars of totally false—and often self-contradictory—premises like, for instance:

1.   Socialism is a mysterious—yet easily avoidable—disease that will befall you, unless you follow the scientific prescription of American modernization;

2.   Facts to the contrary are merely the result of mysterious—yet easily avoidable—mishaps; such facts (e.g., the Russian Revolution of 1917) are devoid of an actual causal foundation and of a wider social-historical significance;

3.   Present-day manifestations of social unrest are merely the combined result of Soviet aspirations and of the absence of American partnership in the societies concerned; therefore, the task is to checkmate the former by generously supplying the latter.

"Theories" resting on such foundations can, of course, amount to no more than the crudest ideological justification for aggressive American expansionism and interventionism. This is why these cynical ideologies of rationalization have to be misrepresented as "objective social and polit-ical science" and the position of those who see through the unctuous advocacy of "seeing the politicians of the early take-off areas through"— by means of the "Great American Partnership" of massive military inter-ventions—must be denounced as "nineteenth-century ideologists."

The moment of truth arrives, however, when the "mishaps" of social explosion occur, even more mysteriously than in the "early take-off areas," in the very land of "supreme modernization" and higher than "high mass-consumption": namely, in America itself. Thus, not only is the model of undisturbed growth and modernization shattered but also, ironically, even the slogan of "sustained growth on a political and social basis which keeps open the possibilities of progressive, democratic devel-opment" ideologically backfires, at a time when outcries against the viola-tion of basic liberties and against the systematic disenfranchising of the masses is on the increase. That we are not talking about some remote, hypothetical future but about our own days goes without saying. What needs stressing, however, is that the dramatic collapse of these pseudo-scientific rationalizations of naked power marks the end of an era: not that of "the end of ideology" but of the end of the almost complete *monopoly* of culture and politics by anti-Marxist ideology, successfully self-adver-tised up until quite recently as the final supersession of all ideology.

2. CAPITALISM AND ECOLOGICAL DESTRUCTION

A decade ago the Walt Rostows of this world were still confidently preaching the *universal* adoption of the American pattern of "high mass-consumption" within the space of one single century. They could not be bothered with making the elementary, but of course necessary, calcula-tions which would have shown them that in the event of the universaliza-tion of that pattern—not to mention the economic, social, and political absurdity of such an idea—the ecological resources of our planet would have been exhausted, several times over, well before the end of that cen-tury. After all, in those days top politicians and their brain trusts did not ride on the bandwagon of ecology but in the sterilized space capsules of astronautical and military fancy. Nothing seemed in those days too big,

too far, and too difficult to those who believed—or wanted us to believe—
in the religion of technological omnipotence and a space odyssey await-
ing around the corner.

Many things have changed in this short decade. The arrogance of military power suffered some severe defeats not only in Vietnam but also in
Cuba and in other parts of the American hemisphere. International power
relations have undergone some significant changes, with the immense
development of China and Japan in the first place, exposing to ridicule
the nicely streamlined calculations of "escalation experts" who now have
to invent not only an entirely new type of multiple-player chess game but
also the kind of creatures willing to play it, for want of real-life takers.
"The affluent society" turned out to be the society of suffocating *effluence,* and its allegedly omnipotent technology failed to cope even with rat
infestation in the slums and ghettos. Nor did the religion of space odyssey
fare any better, notwithstanding the astronomical sums invested in it.
Recently, even the learned Dr. Werner von Braun himself had to link up
the latest version of his irresistible "yearning for the stars" with the prosaic bandwagon of pollution (so far, it seems, without much success).

"The God that failed" in the image of technological omnipotence is
now revarnished and shown around again under the umbrella of universal "ecological concern." Ten years ago ecology could be safely ignored or
dismissed as totally irrelevant. Today, it must be grotesquely misrepresented and one-sidedly exaggerated so that people—sufficiently
impressed by the cataclysmic tone of ecological sermons—can be successfully diverted from their burning social and political problems.
Africans, Asians, and Latin Americans (especially Latin Americans)
should not multiply at pleasure—not even at God's pleasure, if they are
Roman Catholics—for lack of restraint might result in "intolerable ecological strains." That is, in plain words, it might even endanger the prevailing social relations that define the rule of capital. Similarly, people
should forget all about the astronomical expenditure on armaments and
accept sizeable cuts in their standard of living, in order to meet the costs
of "environmental rehabilitation": that is, in plain words, the costs of
keeping the established system of expanding waste production well-oiled.
Not to mention the additional bonus of making people at large pay, under
the pretext of "human survival," for the survival of a socioeconomic sys-

tem, which now has to cope with deficiencies arising from growing international competition and from an increasing shift in favor of the parasitic sectors within its own structure of production.

That capitalism deals in this way with ecology should not surprise us in the least: it would be nothing short of a miracle if it did not. Yet, the exploitation of this issue for the benefit of "the modern industrial state" —to use a nice phrase of Professor Galbraith's—does not mean that we can afford to ignore it. For the problem itself is real enough, whatever use is made of it today.

Indeed, it has been real for quite some time, though, of course, for reasons inherent in the necessity of capitalist growth, few have taken any notice of it. However, Marx—and this should sound incredible only to those who have repeatedly buried him as an "irretrievably irrelevant ideologist of nineteenth-century stamp"—had tackled the issue, within the dimensions of its true social-economic significance, more than one hundred and twenty-five years ago.

Criticizing the abstract and idealist rhetoric with which Feuerbach assessed the relationship between man and nature, Marx wrote:

> Feuerbach . . . always takes refuge in external nature, and moreover in nature which has not yet been subdued by men. But every new invention, every new advance made by industry, detaches another piece from this domain, so that the ground which produces examples illustrating such Feuerbachian propositions is steadily shrinking. The "essence" of the fish is its "existence," water—to go no further than this one proposition. The "essence" of the freshwater fish is the water of a river. But the latter ceases to be the "essence" of the fish and is no longer a suitable medium of existence as soon as the river is made to serve industry, as soon as it is polluted by dyes and other waste products and navigated by steamboats, or as soon as its water is diverted into canals where simple drainage can deprive the fish of its medium of existence.[7]

This is how Marx approached the matter in the early 1840s. Needless to say, he categorically rejected the suggestion that such developments are inevitably inherent in the "human predicament" and that, consequently, the problem is how to *accommodate* ourselves to them in everyday life.[8]

He fully realized, already then, that a radical restructuring of the prevailing *mode* of human interchange and control is the necessary prerequisite to an effective control over the forces of nature, which are brought into motion in a blind and ultimately self-destructive fashion precisely by the prevailing, alienated, and reified mode of human interchange and control. Small wonder, then, that to present-day apologists of the established system of control his prophetic diagnosis is nothing but "parochial anachronism."

To say that "the costs of cleaning up our environment must be met in the end by the community" is both an obvious platitude and a characteristic evasion, although the politicians who sermonize about it seem to believe to have discovered the philosophers' stone. Of course, it is always the community of producers who meet the cost of everything. But the fact that it always *must* meet the costs does not mean in the least that it always *can* do so. Indeed, given the prevailing mode of alienated social control, we can be sure that it *will not be able* to meet them.

Furthermore, to suggest that the already prohibitive costs should be met by "consciously putting aside a certain proportion of the resources derived from extra growth"—at a time of no growth coupled with rising unemployment and rising inflation—is worse than Feuerbach's empty rhetoric. Not to mention the additional problems necessarily inherent in increased capitalistic growth.

And to add that "but this time growth will be controlled growth" is completely beside the point. For the issue is not whether or not we produce under *some* control, but under what *kind* of control; since our present state of affairs has been produced under the "iron-fisted control" of capital, which is envisaged, by our politicians, to remain the fundamental regulating force of our life also in the future.

And, finally, to say that "science and technology *can* solve all our problems in the long run" is much worse than believing in witchcraft; for it tendentiously ignores the devastating social embeddedness of present-day science and technology. In this respect, too, the issue is not whether or not we use science and technology for solving our problems—for obviously we must—but whether or not we *succeed* in radically *changing* their *direction*, which is at present narrowly determined and circumscribed by the self-perpetuating needs of profit maximization.

These are the main reasons why we cannot help being rather skeptical about the present-day institutionalization of these concerns. Mountains are in labor and a mouse is born: the super-institutions of ecological oversight turn out to be rather more modest in their achievements than in their rhetoric of self-justification: namely, ministries for the protection of middle-class amenities.

3. THE CRISIS OF DOMINATION

In the meantime, on this plane as well as on several others, the problems accumulate and the contradictions become increasingly more explosive. The objective tendency inherent in the nature of capital—its growth into a global system coupled with its concentration and increasingly greater technological and science-intensive articulation—undermines and turns into an anachronism the social and structural subordination of labor to capital.[9] Indeed, we can witness already that the traditional forms of hierarchical and structural embeddedness of the functional division of labor tend to disintegrate under the impact of the ever-increasing concentration of capital and socialization of labor. Here, I can merely point to a few indicators of this striking change:

1. The escalating vulnerability of contemporary industrial organization as compared to the nineteenth-century factory. (The so-called wildcat strikes are inconceivable without the underlying economic and technological processes which both induce and enable a "handful" of workers to bring to a halt even a whole branch of industry, with immense potential repercussions.)

2. The economic link up of the various branches of industry into a highly stretched system of closely interdependent parts, with an ever-increasing imperative for safeguarding the *continuity of production* in the system as a whole. (The more the system is stretched, as regards its cycle of reproduction, the greater is the imperative of continuity, and every disturbance leads to more stretch as well as to an ever-darkening shadow of even a temporary

breakdown in continuity.) There are increasingly fewer "peripheral branches," since the repercussions of industrial complications are quickly transferred, in the form of a chain reaction, from any part of the system to all its parts. Consequently, there can be no more "trouble-free industries." The age of paternalistic enterprise has been irretrievably superseded by the rule of "oligopolies" and "super-conglomerates."

3. The growing amount of socially "superfluous time" (or "disposable time"),[10] customarily called "leisure," makes it increasingly absurd, as well as practically impossible, to keep a large section of the population living in apathetic ignorance, divorced from their own intellectual powers. Under the impact of a number of weighty socioeconomic factors the old mystique of intellectual elitism has already disappeared for good. Also, side by side with a growing intellectual unemployment—both potential and actual—as well as a worsening of the cleavage between what one is supposed to be educated for and what one actually finds in employment opportunities, it becomes more and more difficult to maintain the traditional and unquestioning subordination of the vast majority of intellectuals to the authority of capital.

4. The worker as a consumer occupies a position of increasing importance in maintaining the undisturbed run of capitalist production. Yet, he is as completely excluded from control over both production and distribution as ever—as if nothing had happened in the sphere of economics during the last century or two. This is a contradiction, which introduces further complications into the established productive system based on a socially stratified division of labor.

5. The effective establishment of capitalism as an economically interlocking world system greatly contributes to the erosion and disintegration of the traditional, historically formed and locally varying, partial structures of social and political stratification and control, without being able to produce a unified system of control on a worldwide scale. (So long as the power of capital prevails, "world

government" is bound to remain a futurologist pipe dream.) The "crisis of hegemony, or crisis of the state in all spheres" (Gramsci) has become a truly international phenomenon.

In the last analysis all these points are about the question of *social control*. In the course of human development, the function of social control had been alienated from the social body and transferred into capital, which, thus, acquired the power of grouping people in a hierarchical structural and functional pattern, in accordance with the criterion of a greater or lesser share in the necessary control over production and distribution.

There is an objective trend inherent in the development of capital in all spheres—from the mechanical fragmentation of the labor process to the creation of automated systems; from local accumulation of capital to its concentration in the form of an ever-expanding and self-saturating world system; from a partial and local to a comprehensive international division of labor; from limited consumption to an artificially stimulated and manipulated mass-consumption, in the service of an ever-accelerating cycle of reproduction of commodity-society; and from "free time" confined to a privileged few to the mass production of social dynamite, in the form of "leisure," on a universal scale. Ironically, though, this objective trend carries with it a result diametrically opposed to the interest of capital. For in this process of expansion and concentration, the power of control invested in capital is being *de facto* retransferred to the social body as a whole, even if in a necessarily irrational way, thanks to the inherent irrationality of capital itself.

That the objectively slipping control is described from the standpoint of capital as "holding the nation to ransom," does not alter in the least the fact itself. For nineteenth-century capitalism could not be held at ransom even by an army of so-called troublemakers, let alone by a mere handful of them.

Here, we are confronted with the emergence of a fundamental contradiction: that between an effective loss of control and the established form of control, capital. By its very nature, capital can be nothing but control, since it is constituted through an alienated objectification of the function of control, as a reified body apart from and opposed to the social body itself. No wonder, therefore, that in the last few years the idea of workers' control has been gaining in importance in many parts of the world.

The social status quo is rapidly and dramatically disintegrating in front of our very eyes—if only we are willing to open them to see. The distance between Uncle Tom's Cabin and the beleaguered headquarters of black militancy is *astronomical*. And so are the distances from the depressing working-class apathy of the postwar period to today's, even officially admitted, growing militancy on a worldwide scale—from graciously granted presidential "participation" to the Paris street fights; from a badly divided and narrowly wage-orientated Italian trade union movement to the unity necessary for the organization of a political general strike; or, for that matter, from the monolithic, unchallenged rule of Stalinism to the elemental eruption of massive popular dissent in Poland, Hungary, and Czechoslovakia. And yet, it did not take anything like light years—not even light minutes—to travel such astronomical distances.

Not so long ago the "scientific" ideology of gradualist "social engineering"—as opposed to the "religious holism" of revolutionary change and socialism—enjoyed an almost completely monopolistic position not only in educational and cultural institutions but also in the ante-chambers of political power. But, good heavens, what are we witnessing today? The dramatic announcement of the need for a "major revolution" by none other than President Nixon himself, in his recent State of the Union message; followed by the Shah of Persia's warning that he is going to spearhead the "rebellion of the have-nots against the haves."

And Mr. Wilson too, who mysteriously lost the word "socialism" from his vocabulary the very minute he walked through the front door of 10 Downing Street—and it could not be found, though his entire team of experts and advisers as well as cabinet colleagues were looking for it for almost six years through the powerful spectacles of "pragmatic modernization," supplied completely free of prescription charges—mysteriously found the word again after leaving the Prime Ministerial residence by the back door. Indeed, in one of his public speeches he even cracked a joke about the "Pentagon hunting for communists under the seabed," though, at the same time, by a slight fit of amnesia forgetting that he was himself fishing for communists under the Seamen's bed not that long ago.

President Nixon: a new *revolutionary*; the Shah of Persia: *leader of the world rebellion of the have-nots*; and Mr. Wilson: an indomitable *crusader against the Pentagon's anti-communist crusades*. I wonder what might come next. (I did not have to wonder for long. Only a few days after this lecture was delivered, Mr. Heath—yet another "pragmatic modernizer," of Rolls Royce fame—hastened to add, in the truest spirit of consensus politics, his name to our illustrious list: as a vigorous *champion of nationalization*.)

However, even metamorphoses of this kind are indicative of powerful pressures whose nature simply cannot be grasped through the mystifying personalization of the issues as expressed in hollow concepts like "bridging the credibility gap" or "acquiring a new image." The hypothesis that politicians break their promises because they are "devious" and "lack integrity" only begs the question, at best. And the suggestion that they change their slogans and catchphrases, because "they need to change their image" is the emptiest of the whole range of tautologies produced by the postwar boom of behaviorist and functionalist "political science." Concepts of this kind are nothing more than pretentiously inflated rationalizations for the practice of self-advertising through which the advertising media sell their services to credulous politicians. As Mr. Wilson himself can testify, the simple and strictly quantifiable truth is that the psephologist's "credibility gap" between this kind of "scientific" electoral victory forecast and the painfully final result of defeat exactly equals the distance between the front door and the back door of 10 Downing Street.

If the tone of traditional politics is changing today, it is because the objective contradictions of our present-day situation cannot be repressed any longer, either by means of naked power and brute force or through the soft strangulation supplied by consensus politics. Yet, what we are confronted with is but an unprecedented crisis of social control on a world scale, and not its solution. It would be highly irresponsible to lull ourselves into a state of euphoria, contemplating a "socialist world revolution round the corner."

The power of capital, in its various forms of manifestation, though far from being exhausted, no longer reaches far enough. Capital operates on the basis of the myopic rationality of narrow self-interest—of *bellum omnium contra omnes*: the war of each against all. As such, capital is a mode of control that is *a priori* incapable of providing the comprehensive rationality of an adequate social control. And it is precisely the need for the latter which demonstrates its dramatic urgency with the passing of every day.

The awareness of the limits of capital has been absent from all forms of rationalization of its reified needs, not only from the more recent versions of capitalist ideology. Paradoxically, however, capital is now forced to take notice of some of these limits, although, of course, in a necessarily alienated form. For now, at least, the absolute limits of human existence—both on the military and the ecological plane—*must* be sized up, no matter how distorting and mystifying the measuring devices of a capitalist socioeconomic accountancy may be. Facing the danger of nuclear annihilation on one side and the irreversible destruction of the human environment on the other, it becomes imperative to devise practical alternatives and remedies whose failure is rendered inevitable by the very limits of capital, which have now collided with the limits of human existence itself.

The limits of capital, it goes without saying, carry with them an approach that tries to exploit even these vital human concerns in the service of profit making. The lunatic—but, of course, capitalistically "rational"—theories (and associated practices) of "escalating" war industry as the ultimate safeguard against war have dominated "strategic thinking" now for quite some time. And recently we could observe the mushrooming of parasitic enterprises—from the smallest to the largest in size—which all try to cash in on our growing awareness of the ecological dangers. (Not to mention the ideological and political operations associated with the same issues.[11])

All the same, such manipulations do not resolve the issues at stake. They can only contribute to their further aggravation. Capitalism and the rationality of comprehensive social planning are radically incompatible. Today, however, we witness the emergence of a fundamental contradiction, with the gravest possible implications for the future of capitalism: for the first time in human history the unhampered dominance and expansion of the inherently irrational capitalist structures and mechanisms of social control are being seriously interfered with by pressures arising from the elementary imperatives of mere survival. And since the issues themselves are as unavoidable as the contradiction between the need for an adequate social control and the narrow limits of capitalist accountancy is sharp, the necessary failure of programs of shortsighted manipulation—in a situation which demands far-reaching and consciously coordinated efforts on a massive scale—acts as a catalyst for the development of socialist alternatives.

And this is far from being the sum total of the rising complications. The mass production of disposable time mentioned earlier is now coupled not only with expanding knowledge, but also with growing consciousness of the contradictions inherent in the practically demonstrated failures, as well as with the development of new modes and means of communication potentially *capable* of bringing to light the massive evidence for the eruption of these contradictions.[12]

At the same time, some of the most fundamental institutions of society are affected by a crisis never even imagined before.

The power of religion in the West has almost completely evaporated, but this fact has been masked by the persistence of its rituals and, above all, by the effective functioning of substitute-religions, from the abstract cult of "thrift" in the more remote past to the religion of "consumer sovereignty" and "technological omnipotence" in more recent decades.

The structural crisis of education has been in evidence now for a number of years. And it is getting deeper every day, although its intensification does not necessarily take the form of spectacular confrontations.

And the most important of them all: the virtual *disintegration* of the present-day family—this cell of class society—presents a challenge to which there cannot conceivably be formal and institutional answers, whether in the form of "amending the law of trespass" or in some more ruthlessly repressive form. The crisis of this institution assumes many forms of manifestation, from the hippie cults to widespread drug use; from the Women's Liberation Movement to the establishment of utopian enclaves of communal living; and from the much advertised "generational conflict" to the most disciplined and militant manifestations of that conflict in organized action. Those who have laughed at them in the past had better think again. For whatever might be their relative weight in the total picture today, they are potentially of the greatest significance.

Equally significant is the way in which the stubborn persistence of wishful thinking misidentifies the various forms of crisis. Not only are the manifestations of conflict ignored up to the last minute; they are also misrepresented the minute after the last. When they cannot be swept any longer under the carpet, they are tackled merely as *effects* divorced from their *causes*. (We should remember the absurd hypotheses of "mysterious diseases" and of "events devoid of any foundation" mentioned above.)

Characteristically, we find in a recent book on economics, at the foot of a page which calls for "reducing industrial investments in favour of a large-scale re-planning of our cities, and of restoring and enhancing the beauty of many of our villages, towns and resorts," the following story:

> The recent electric-power breakdown in New York, obviously to be deplored on grounds of efficiency, broke the spell of monotony for millions of New Yorkers. People enjoyed the shock of being thrown back on their innate resources and into sudden dependence upon one another. For a few hours people were freed from routine and brought together by the dark. Next-door strangers spoke, and were gladdened to help each other. There was room for kindness. The fault was repaired. The genie of power was returned to each home. And as the darkness brought them stumbling into each other's arms, so *the hard light scattered them again.* Yet someone was quoted as saying, "This should happen at least once a month."[13]

The only thing one does not quite understand: why not at least once a week? Surely the immense savings on all that unused electricity would more than cover the costs of a "large-scale re-planning of our cities, and of restoring and enhancing the beauty of many of our villages, towns and resorts." Not to mention the supreme benefits inherent in practicing the newfound virtue of unlit-skyscraper-corridor-brotherhood on a weekly basis. Apparently it is not the mode of their social relationships that "scatters people" apart, but the technological efficiency and monotony of "hard light." Thus, the obvious remedy is to give them less hard light and all the unwanted problems disappear for good. That the production of hard light is a social necessity, and cannot be replaced even for the duration of periodic rituals by soft candlelight, is a consideration evidently unworthy of the attention of our champions in romantic daydreaming.

To put it in another way: such wishful thinking is characterized by a curt dismissal of all those expectations that the system cannot meet. The representatives of this approach insist, with unfailing tautology, that such expectations are not the manifestation of social and economic contradictions but merely the *effects* of "rising expectations." Thus, not only is the challenge of facing up to the *causal foundations* of frustrated expectations systematically evaded but also this evasion itself is very conveniently rationalized.

The fact is, however, that we are concerned here with an internal contradiction of a system of production and control: one which cannot help raising expectations, even to the point of a complete breakdown in satisfying them. And it is precisely at such points of breakdown that quixotic remedies and substitutes are advocated with so much "humanitarian" passion. Up until these points of crisis and breakdown, no one in her right mind is supposed to question the superior wisdom of "cost-effectiveness," "business sense," "technological efficiency," and "economic motives." But no sooner does the system fail to deliver the goods it so loudly advertised the moment before—confidently indicating, prior to the eruption of structural disturbances, its own ability to cater to expanding expectations as the self-evident proof of its superiority over all possible alternative modes of production and social control—its apologists immediately switch from preaching the religion of "cost-effectiveness" and "economic motives" to sermonizing about the need for "self-denial" and "idealism," untroubled not only by their sudden change of course but also by the rhetorical unreality of their wishful "solutions."

Thus, beyond the horizon of "artificial obsolescence" we are suddenly confronted with "theories" advocating the planning of artificial power cuts, the production of artificial scarcity—both material and as an antidote to too much "disposable time" which involves the danger of an increasing social consciousness; of space-solidarity and artificially manipulated suspense. Indeed, at a time of dangerously rising unemployment, there are still with us antediluvian "theorists" who wish to counteract the complications arising from a total lack of purpose in saturated commodity-existence by seriously advocating the production of artificial unemployment and hardship, topping it all off with nostalgic speeches about lost religions and the need for a new artificial religion. The only thing they

fail to reveal is how they plan to devise an artificial being who will systematically fail to notice these grotesque artificialities.

Once upon a time it suited the development of capitalism to let out of
the bottle the genie of the ruthless conversion of everything into mar-
ketable commodities, even though this deed necessarily carried with it the
undermining and the ultimate disintegration of religious, political, and
educational institutions which were vital to the control mechanism of class
society. Today, however, the status quo would be much better served by a
restoration of all the undermined and disintegrating institutions of control.
According to our romantic critics, everything would be well if only the
genie could be persuaded to retire back into the bottle. The trouble is,
though, that he has no intention whatsoever of doing so. Thus, nothing
much remains for our romantics except lamenting upon the wickedness of
the genie and upon the folly of the human beings who let him loose.

4. FROM "REPRESSIVE TOLERANCE" TO THE LIBERAL ADVOCACY OF REPRESSION

When the system fails to cope with the manifestations of dissent, while at
the same time it is incapable of dealing with their causal foundations, not
only do fantasy figures and remedies appear on the stage but also the
"realists" of a repressive rejection of all criticism.

In 1957 a gifted young writer, Conrad Reinhold, had to flee East
Germany where he used to run a political cabaret in the aftermath of the
Twentieth Congress. After he had some experience of life in West
Germany, he was asked in an interview published in *Der Spiegel*,[14] to
describe the main difference between his old and new situation. This was
his answer: "*Im Osten soll das Kabarett die Gesellschaft ändern, darf aber
nichts sagen; im Western kann es alles sagen, darf aber nichts ändern.*" (In
the East the political cabaret is supposed to change society, but it is not
allowed to say anything; in the West it is allowed to say whatever it pleases, but it is not allowed to change anything.)

This example illustrates quite well the dilemma of social control. For
the other side of the coin of "*repressive* tolerance" is the "*repression* of tolerance." The two together mark the limits of social systems that are inca-

pable of meeting the need for social change in a determinate historical period.

When Marx died in 1883, his death was reported in *The Times* with some delay.[15] And no wonder: for it had to be reported to the London *Times* from *Paris* that Marx had died in *London*. And this, again, illustrates very well our dilemma. For it is easy to be liberal even when even a Marx can be totally ignored, since his voice cannot be heard where he lives, thanks to the political and ideological vacuum that surrounds him. But what happens when the rising pressure of the ever-increasing social contradictions displaces the political vacuum? Will not, in that case, the frustrations generated by the necessary failure of attending only to the surface manifestations of socioeconomic troubles, instead of tackling their causes, take refuge behind a show of strength, even if this means the violation of the selfsame liberal values in whose name the violation is now committed? The recent case of another young refugee from East Germany—this time not a political cabaret writer but someone deeply concerned about the degradation of politics to the level of cheap cabaret, Rudi Dutschke— suggests a rather disturbing answer to our question.

The issue is not that of "personal aberration" or "political pigheadedness," as some commentators saw it. Unfortunately, it is much worse than that: namely, an ominous attempt to bring the political organs of control in line with the needs of the present-day articulation of the capitalist economy, even if such an adjustment requires a "liberal" transition from "repressive tolerance" to "repressive intolerance." Those who continue to nurse illusions about these matters should read their allegedly impartial daily paper somewhat more attentively, in order to grasp the carefully woven meaning of passages like this:

> The harder the liberal university is pressed, the less comprehensive it can *afford* to be, the more rigorously will it have to draw the line, and the more likely will be the *exclusion of intolerant points of view*. The paradox of the *tolerant society* is that it cannot be defended solely by *tolerant* means just as the *pacific society* cannot be defended solely by peaceful means.[16]

As we can see, the empty myths of "the tolerant society" and "the pacific society" are used to describe the society of *bellum omnium contra omnes.* Such myths disregard the painfully obvious ways in which the "pacific society" of U.S. capitalism demonstrates its true character by saturation bombing, wholesale slaughter, and massacres in Vietnam, and by shooting down even its own youth in front of the "liberal university"—in Kent State and elsewhere—when they dare to mount a protest against the unspeakable inhumanities of this "tolerant" and "pacific" society.

Moreover, in such passages of editorial wisdom we can notice the unintended acknowledgment of the fact that this "liberal" and "tolerant" society is tolerant only to a certain point—i.e., not beyond the point at which protest starts to become effective and turns into a genuine social challenge to the perpetuation of the society of repressive tolerance. As well, we can notice the sophisticated hypocrisy through which the advocacy of *crude* ("rigorous") and *institutionalized intolerance* ("exclusion") succeeds in representing itself as the liberal defense of society against "intolerant points of view."

Similarly, the advocacy of institutionalized intolerance is extended to prescribing "solutions" to trade union disputes. Another *Times* article—significantly entitled "*A Battle Line at 10 per cent*"[17]—concedes that "nobody knows for sure what the mechanism which causes . . . runaway inflation is" and murmurs something about the fate of "some sort of authoritarian regime," which befalls the countries with substantial inflation. It then goes on to advocate blatantly authoritarian measures:

> What can be done to reverse the present inflationary trend? The first and immediate answer is that the country should recognize the justice of *standing firm.* Anyone in present circumstances who asks for more than 10 per cent is joining in a process of self-destruction. Anyone who strikes because he will not accept 15 per cent deserves to be resisted with all the influence of society and *all the power of government. . . .*[18] *The first thing to do and the simplest is to start beating strikes.* [!!!] The local authorities should be given *total support* [including troops?] in refusing to make any further offer, *even if the strike lasts for months.*

We can see, then, that the *apparent* concern about the (fictitious) danger of "some sort of authoritarian regime"—which is simply declared to be inevitably linked to major inflations—is only a cover for the real concern about protecting the interests of capital, no matter how grave the political implications of "standing firm" against "strikes lasting for months" might be. To formulate, thus, the highest priorities in terms of "beating the strikes" is and remains *authoritarian,* even if policy based on such measures is championed in editorial columns capable of assuming liberal positions on peripheral issues.

After the advocacy of institutionalized intolerance, in the form of "beating the strikes with all the power of government," the legitimation of such practices through *anti-union laws,* is, of course, only the next logical step. And the record of consensus politics is particularly telling in this respect.[19] For Mrs. Castle's denunciation of the Tory anti-union bill is not just halfhearted and belated. It also suffers from the memory of its twin brother—the ill-fated Labour bill—for which she could certainly not disclaim maternity. And when Mrs. Castle writes about *The Bad Bosses' Charter,*[20] she merely highlights the stubborn illusions of "pragmatic" politicians who, notwithstanding their past experience, still imagine that they will be voted back into office in order to write in the statute books a charter for the good bosses.

From a socialist point of view, bosses are neither "bad" nor "good." Just *bosses.* And that is bad enough: in fact, it could not be worse. This is why it is vital to go beyond the paralyzing limits of consensus politics, which refuses to recognize this elementary truth, and makes the people at large pay for the disastrous consequences of its mounting failures.

5. "WAR IF THE NORMAL METHODS OF EXPANSION FAIL"

Under the devastating impact of a shrinking rate of profit, which must be monopolistically counteracted, the margin of traditional political action has been reduced to slavishly carrying out the dictates arising from the most urgent and immediate demands of capital-expansion, even if such operations are invariably misrepresented as "the national interest" by both sides of the "national" consensus.[21] And just how directly policymaking is subordinated to the dictates of monopoly capital— unceremoniously excluding the vast majority of the elected representatives from the determination of all the important matters—is revealed in most unexpected ways by such embarrassing events as the headline-catching resignation of supposedly key decision-makers: some members of the most exclusive "inner cabinets" (restricted to a mere handful of ministers) who protest that they had no say in deciding the crucial issues of their own departments, let alone the national policy as a whole.

Even more revealing is the meteoric rise of the self-appointed representatives of big business and high finance to the top of political decision-making. The state, at a time of an already enormous but still extending concentration of capital, is assigned the vital role of sustaining, with all available means at its disposal, the capitalist system of production. So much is at stake that the traditional forms of indirect (economic) control of policy-making must be abandoned in favor of *direct* control of the "commanding heights" of politics by the spokespersons of monopoly capital. In contrast to such manifestations of actual economic and political developments, which we have all witnessed in the recent past and are still witnessing today, the mythology of realizing socialist ideals by pragmatically acquiring control over the commanding heights of a mixed economy must sound particularly hollow indeed.

Thus, politics—which is nothing unless it is a conscious application of strategic measures capable of profoundly affecting social development as a whole—is turned into a mere instrument of shortsighted manipulation, completely devoid of any comprehensive plan and design of its own. It is condemned to follow a pattern of belated and short-term reactive moves to the bewildering crisis-events as they necessarily erupt, with increasing frequency, on the socioeconomic basis of self-saturating commodity production and self-stultifying capital accumulation.

The crisis we face, then, is not simply a political crisis, but the general structural crisis of the capitalistic institutions of social control in their entirety. Here, the main point is that the institutions of capitalism are inherently violent and aggressive: they are built on the fundamental premise of "war if the 'normal' methods of expansion fail." (Besides, the periodic *destruction*—by whatever means, including the most violent ones— of overproduced capital, is an inherent necessity of the "normal" functioning of this system: the vital condition of its recovery from crisis and depression.) The blind "natural law" of the market mechanism carries

with it the consequence that the grave social problems necessarily associated with capital production and concentration are never *solved*, only
postponed, and indeed—since postponement cannot work indefinitely—
transferred to the *military* plane. Thus, the "sense" of the hierarchically
structured institutions of capitalism is given in its ultimate reference to the
violent "fighting out" of the issues, in the international arena. For the
socioeconomic units—following the inner logic of their development—
grow bigger and bigger, and their problems and contradictions increasingly more intense and grave. Growth and expansion are immanent
necessities of the capitalist system of production, and when the local limits are reached there is no way out except by violently readjusting the prevailing relation of forces.

The capitalist system of our time, however, has been decapitated
through the removal of its ultimate sanction: an all-out war on its real or
potential adversaries. Exporting internal violence is no longer possible on
the required massive scale. (Attempts at doing so on a limited scale—e.g.,
the Vietnam War—are not substitutes for the old mechanism and even
accelerate the inevitable internal explosions, by aggravating the inner contradictions of the system.) Nor is it possible to get away indefinitely with
the ideological mystifications which represented the *internal* challenge of
socialism, the only possible solution to the present crisis of social control,
as an *external* confrontation: a "subversion" directed from abroad by a
"monolithic" enemy. For the first time in history capitalism is globally
confronted with its own problems, which cannot be "postponed" much
longer. Nor, indeed, can they be transferred to the military plane in order
to be "exported" in the form of an all-out war.

Blocking the road of a possible solution to the grave structural crisis
of society through a third world war is of immense significance as far as
the future development of capitalism is concerned. The grave implications of this blockage can be grasped by remembering that the "Great
Wars" of the past:

1. automatically "dematerialized" the capitalist system of incentives
    (producing a shift from "economic motives" to the "self-denial" and
    "idealism" so dear to the heart of some recent spokesmen and apol-
    ogists of the system in trouble), adjusting, accordingly, the mecha-

nism of "interiorization" through which the continued legitimation of the established order is successfully accomplished;

2.   suddenly imposed a radically lower standard of living on the masses of people, who willingly accepted it, given the circumstances of a state of emergency;

3.   with equal suddenness radically widened the formerly depressed margin of profit;

4.   introduced a vital element of rationalization and coordination into the system as a whole (a rationalization, which, thanks to the extraordinary circumstances, did not have to be confined to the narrow limits of all rationalization that directly arises from the sole needs of capital production and expansion);

5.   gave an immense technological boost to the economy as a whole, on a wide front.

Current military demand, however massive, simply cannot be compared to this set of both economic and ideological factors whose removal may well prove too much for the system of world capitalism. Present-day military demand—which is imposed on society under "peacetime" conditions and not under those of a "national emergency"—cannot help intensifying the contradictions of capital production. This fact is powerfully highlighted by the spectacular failures of companies which depend heavily for their survival on mammoth defense contracts (Lockheed and Rolls Royce, for instance).

The issue is, however, far more fundamental than even the most spectacular of failures could adequately indicate. For it concerns the structure of present-day capitalist production as a whole, and not simply one of its branches. Nor could one reasonably expect the state to solve the problem, no matter how much public money is poured down the drain in the course of its revealing rescue operations.

Indeed, it was the tendency of increasing state interventions in economic matters in the service of capital-expansion which led to the present state of affairs in the first place. The result of such interventions was not only the cancerous growth of the non-productive branches of industry within the total framework of capital production but also the grave distortion of the whole structure of *capitalist cost-accounting* under the impact of contracts carried out with the ideological justification that they were "vital to the national interest." Since present-day capitalism constitutes a closely *interlocking system,* the devastating results of this structural distortion come to the fore in numerous fields and branches of industry, and not only in those which are *directly* involved in the execution of defense contracts. The well-known facts that original cost-estimates as a rule madly "escalate" and that the committees set up by governments in order to "scrutinize" them fail to produce results (that is, results other than the whitewashing of past operations, coupled with generous justifications of future outlays) find their explanation in the immanent necessities of this changed structure of capitalist production and accountancy, with the gravest implications for the future.

Thus, the power of state intervention in the economy—not so long ago still widely believed to be the wonder drug of all conceivable ills and troubles of "modern industrial society"—is strictly confined to accelerating the maturation of these contradictions. The larger the dose administered to the convalescing patient, the greater is the dependency on the wonder drug. That is, the graver the symptoms described above as the structural distortion of the whole system of capitalist cost accounting. These symptoms menacingly foreshadow the ultimate paralysis and breakdown of the mechanisms of capital production and expansion. And the fact that what is supposed to be the remedy turns out to be a contributory cause of further crisis clearly demonstrates that we are not concerned here with some "passing dysfunction" but with a fundamental, dynamic contradiction of the whole structure of capital production at its historic phase of decline and ultimate disintegration.

6. THE EMERGENCE OF CHRONIC UNEMPLOYMENT

Equally important is the newly emerging pattern of unemployment. In recent decades, unemployment in the highly developed capitalist countries has been largely confined to "pockets of underdevelopment." The fact that it affected millions of people used to be optimistically written off, in the grand style of neo-capitalist self-complacency, as one of the "inevitable costs of modernization," without too much—if any—worry about the social-economic repercussions of the trend itself.

Insofar as the prevailing movement was from unskilled to *skilled* jobs, involving large sums of capital outlay in industrial development, the matter could be ignored with relative safety, in the midst of the euphoria of "expansion." Under such circumstances the human misery necessarily associated with all types of unemployment—including the misery produced in the interest of "modernization"—could be capitalistically justified in the name of a bright commodity-buying future for everyone. In those days, the unfortunate millions of apathetic and "underprivileged" people could easily be relegated to the periphery of society. Isolated as a social phenomenon from the rest of the "Great Society" of affluence, they were expected to blame only their own "uselessness" (want of skill, lack of "drive," and so forth) for their predicament and to consume, in resignation, the leftovers of the heavily laden neo-capitalist dinner table, magnanimously dished out in the form of unemployment "benefits" and surplus-food coupons. (We should not forget that, in those days, some of the most prominent economists were seriously advocating programs which would have institutionalized—in the name of "technological progress" and "cost-efficiency"—the permanent condemnation of a major proportion of the labor force to the brutally dehumanizing existence of enforced idleness and total dependence on "social charity.")

What was systematically ignored, however, was the fact that the trend of capitalist "modernization" and the displacement of large amounts of unskilled labor, in preference to a much smaller amount of skilled labor, ultimately implied the *reversal* of the trend itself: namely, the breakdown of "modernization," coupled with massive unemployment. This fact of the utmost gravity simply *had* to be ignored, in that its recognition is radically incompatible with the continued acceptance of the capitalist perspective of social control. For the underlying dynamic contradiction, which leads to the drastic reversal of the trend, is by no means inherent in the *technology* employed, but in the blind subordination of both *labor and technology* to the devastatingly narrow limits of capital as the supreme arbiter of social development and control.

To acknowledge, though, the social embeddedness of the given technology would have amounted to admitting the socioeconomic limitations of the capitalist applications of technology. This is why the apologists of the capitalist relations of production had to theorize about "growth," "development," and "modernization" *as such,* instead of assessing the sobering *limits* of *capitalist* growth and development. This is why they had to talk about the "affluent," "modern industrial"—or indeed "post-industrial"—and "consumer" society as such, instead of the artificial, contradictory affluence of *waste-producing commodity-society*, which relies for its "modern industrial" cycle of reproduction not only on the most cynical manipulation of "consumer demand" but also on the most callous exploitation of the "have-nots."

Although there is no reason why *in principle* the trend of moderniza-tion and the displacement of unskilled by skilled labor should not go on indefinitely, as far as *technology itself* is concerned, there is a very good reason why this trend must be reversed under capitalist relations of pro-duction: namely, the catastrophically restricting criteria of profitability and expansion of exchange-value to which such "modernization" is nec-essarily subordinated. Thus, the newly emerging pattern of unemploy-ment as a socioeconomic trend is, again, indicative of the deepening structural crisis of present-day capitalism.

In accordance with this trend, the problem is no longer just the plight of unskilled laborers but also that of large numbers of *highly skilled* work-ers, who are now chasing, in addition to the earlier pool of unemployed, the depressingly few available jobs. Also, the trend of "rationalizing" amputation is no longer confined to the "peripheral branches of ageing industry" but embraces some of the *most developed* and modernized sec-tors of production—from shipbuilding and aviation to electronics and from engineering to space technology.

Thus, we are no longer concerned with the "normal," and willingly accepted, byproducts of "growth and development" but with their driv-ing to a halt; nor are we concerned with the peripheral problems of "pockets of underdevelopment" but with a fundamental contradiction of the capitalist mode of production as a whole, which turns even the latest achievements of "development," "rationalization" and "modernization" into the paralyzing burden of chronic underdevelopment. Most important of all, the human agency, which finds itself at the receiving end, is no longer the socially powerless, apathetic, and fragmented multitude of "underprivileged" people but *all* categories of skilled and unskilled labor: i.e., objectively, the *total labor force* of society.

We are talking about a major *trend* of social development, and not about some mechanical determinism that announces the immediate collapse of world capitalism. But even though the storehouse of manipulative countermeasures is far from being exhausted, no such measure is capable of suppressing the trend itself in the long run. Whatever might be the rate of success of measures arising from, or compatible with, the basic requirements and limitations of the capitalist mode of production, the crucial fact is and remains that under the present-day circumstances and conditions of capital production the totality of the labor force is becoming involved in an ever-intensifying confrontation with monopoly capital—which carries far-reaching consequences for the development of social consciousness.

7. THE INTENSIFICATION OF THE RATE OF EXPLOITATION

Here we can see, again, the vital importance of blocking the road of possible solutions to the structural crisis of capitalism through the violent displacement of its problems in the form of a new world war. Under the changed circumstances some of the most powerful instruments of mystification—through which capital managed to exercise its paralyzing ideological control over labor in the past—become dangerously undermined and tend to collapse altogether. For now the immense tensions generated within the system of capital production cannot be exported on an adequately massive scale at the expense of other countries. Thus, the basic social antagonism between capital and labor, which lies at the roots of such tensions, cannot be sealed down indefinitely: *the contradictions must be fought out at the place where they are actually generated.*

Capital, when it reaches a point of saturation in its own setting and, at the same time, cannot find outlets for further expansion through the vehicle of imperialism and neo-colonialism, has no alternative but to make its own indigenous labor force suffer the grave consequences of the deteriorating rate of profit. Accordingly, the working classes of some of the most developed "post-industrial" societies are getting a foretaste of the real viciousness of "liberal" capital.

The interplay of a number of major factors—from the dramatic development of the forces of production to the erection of enormous obstacles to the unhampered international expansion of monopoly capital—have exposed and undermined the mechanism of the traditional double bookkeeping which in the past enabled capital to conform to the rules of liberalism at home while practicing and perpetuating the most brutal forms of authoritarianism abroad. Thus, the real nature of the capitalist production relations: the ruthless domination of labor by capital is becoming increasingly more evident as a *global* phenomenon.

Indeed, it could not be otherwise. For so long as the problems of labor are assessed merely in *partial* terms (i.e., as *local* issues of fragmented, stratified, and divided groups of workers) they remain a mystery for theory, and nothing but cause for chronic frustration for politically-minded social practice.

The understanding of the development and self-reproduction of the capitalist mode of production is quite impossible without the concept of the *total* social capital, which alone can explain many mysteries of commodity-society—from the "average rate of profit" to the laws governing capital-expansion and concentration. Similarly, it is quite impossible to understand the manifold and thorny problems of nationally varying, as well as socially stratified labor, without constantly keeping in mind the necessary framework for a proper assessment: namely, the irreconcilable antagonism between *total* social capital and the *totality* of labor.

This fundamental antagonism, it goes without saying, is inevitably modified in accordance with: (1) the local socioeconomic circumstances; (2) the respective positions of particular countries in the global framework of capital production; (3) the relative maturity of global socio-historical development.

Accordingly, at different periods of time, the system as a whole reveals the workings of a complex set of objective differences of interest on *both* sides of the social antagonism. The objective reality of different *rates of exploitation*—both within a given country and in the world system of monopoly capital—is as unquestionable as the objective difference in the *rates of profit* at any particular time. Ignorance of such differences can only result in resounding rhetoric, instead of revolutionary strategies. All the same, the reality of the different rates of exploitation and profit does not alter in the least the fundamental law itself: i.e., the growing *equalization* of the differential rates of exploitation as the *global trend* of development of world capital.

To be sure, this law of equalization is a long-term trend as far as the global system of capital is concerned. Nevertheless, modifications of the system as a whole also appear, already in the short run, as "disturbances" of a particular economy that happens to be negatively affected by the repercussions of the shifts which necessarily occur within the global framework of total social capital.

The dialectic of such shifts and modifications is extremely complex and cannot be pursued, at this point, much further. Let it now suffice to say that "total social capital" should not be confused with "total national capital." When the latter is being affected by a relative weakening of its position within the global system, it will inevitably try to compensate for its losses by increasing its specific rate of exploitation over and against the labor force under its direct control—or else its competitive position is further weakened within the global framework of "total social capital." Under the system of capitalist social control there can be no way out from such "short-term disturbances and dysfunctions" other than the intensification of the specific rates of exploitation, which can only lead, both locally and in global terms, to an explosive intensification of the fundamental social antagonism in the long run.

Those who have been talking about the "integration" of the working class—depicting "organized capitalism" as a system which succeeded in radically mastering its social contradictions—have hopelessly misidentified the manipulative success of the differential rates of exploitation (which prevailed in the relatively "disturbance-free" historic phase of postwar reconstruction and expansion) as a basic *structural remedy*.

As a matter of fact, it was nothing of the kind. The ever-increasing frequency with which "temporary disturbances and dysfunctions" appear in all spheres of our social existence, and the utter failure of manipulative measures and instruments devised to cope with them, are clear evidence that the structural crisis of the capitalist mode of social control has assumed all-embracing proportions.

8. CAPITAL'S "CORRECTIVES" AND
SOCIALIST CONTROL

The manifest failure of established institutions and their guardians to cope with our problems can only intensify the explosive dangers of a deadlock. And this takes us back to our point of departure: the imperative of an adequate social control, which humanity needs for its sheer survival.

To recognize this need is not the same thing as issuing an invitation to indulge in the production of "practicable" blueprints of socioeconomic readjustment in the spirit of accommodating liberal meliorism. Those who usually lay down the criterion of practicability as the measure of seriousness of social criticism hypocritically hide the fact that their real measure, in terms of which the practicability of all programs of action is to be evaluated, is the capitalist mode of production.

Practicable *in relation to what?* That is the question. For if the criteria of capital production constitute the "neutral" basis of all evaluation, then, of course, no socialist program can stand the test of this "value-free," "nonideological" and "objective" approach. This is why Marx himself who insisted that men must change "from top to bottom the conditions of their industrial and political existence, and consequently *their whole manner of being*," must be condemned as a hopelessly impractical ideologist.[22] For how could men conceivably change from top to bottom the conditions of their existence if conformity to the conditions of capital production remains the necessary premise of all admissible change?

And yet, when the very existence of mankind is at stake, as indeed it happens to be at this juncture of an unprecedented crisis in human history, the only program which is really practicable—in sharp contrast to the counterproductive practicality of manipulative measures which only aggravate the crisis—is the Marxian program of radically restructuring, from top to bottom, the totality of social institutions, the industrial, political, and ideological conditions of present-day existence, and the whole manner of being of men and women repressed by the alienated and reified conditions of commodity-society. Short of the realization of such "impracticability," there can be no way out from the ever-deepening crisis of human existence.

The demand for practicable blueprints is the manifestation of a desire to integrate the "constructive" elements of social criticism; a desire coupled with the determination to devise ruthlessly effective countermeasures against those elements which resist integration and are, therefore, *a priori* defined as "destructive." But even if this were not so: truly adequate programs and instruments of sociopolitical action can only be elaborated by critical and self-critical social practice itself, in the course of the actual development of such practice.

Thus, the socialist institutions of social control cannot define themselves *in detail* prior to their practical articulation. At this point of historic transition, the relevant questions concern their general character and direction: determined, in the first place, by the prevailing mode and institutions of control to which they have to constitute a radical alternative. Accordingly, the central characteristics of the new mode of social control can be concretely identified—to a degree to which this is necessary for the elaboration and implementation of flexible socialist strategies—through the grasp of the basic functions and inherent contradictions of the disintegrating system of social control.[23]

Here, we must confine ourselves to mentioning only the most important points—among them the relationship between politics and economics in the first place. As is well known, Marx's bourgeois critics never ceased to accuse him of "economic determinism." Nothing, however, could be further from the truth. For the Marxian program is formulated precisely as the *emancipation* of human action from the power of relentless economic determinations.

Marx demonstrated that the brute force of economic determinism, set into motion by the dehumanizing necessities of capital production, rules over all aspects of human life. He also demonstrated, at the same time, the inherently *historical*—i.e., necessarily *transient*—character of the prevailing mode of production. As such, he touched upon a sore point of bourgeois ideology: the hollowness of its metaphysical belief in the "natural

law" of the permanence of the given production relations. And by revealing the inherent contradictions of this mode of production, Marx demonstrated the necessary *breakdown* of its objective economic determinism.
Such a breakdown, however, had to consummate itself by extending the
power of capital to its extreme limits, submitting absolutely everything —
including the supposedly autonomous power of political decision-making—to its own mechanism of strict control.

Ironically, though, when this is accomplished (as a result of an
increasingly bigger appetite for "correctives" devised to safeguard the
unhampered expansion of the power of capital), monopoly capital is compelled to assume direct control over areas that it is structurally incapable
of controlling. Thus, beyond a certain point, the more it controls (directly), the less it controls (effectively), undermining and eventually destroying even the mechanisms of "correctives." The complete and by now
overt subordination of politics to the most immediate dictates of capital-
producing economic determinism is a vital aspect of this problematic.
This is why the road to the establishment of the new institutions of social
control must lead through a *radical emancipation of politics from the
power of capital.*

Another basic contradiction of the capitalist system of control is that
it cannot separate "advance" from *destruction,* nor "progress" from
waste—however catastrophic the results. The more it unlocks the powers
of productivity, the more it must unleash the powers of destruction; and
the more it extends the volume of production, the more it must bury
everything under mountains of suffocating waste. The concept of *economy* is radically incompatible with the "economy" of capital production. It
adds insult to injury by first using up with rapacious wastefulness the *limited resources* of our planet and then further aggravates the outcome by
polluting and poisoning the human environment with its mass-produced
waste and effluence.

Ironically, though, the system breaks down at the point of its supreme
power; for its maximum extension inevitably generates the vital need for
restraint and conscious control with which capital production is structurally incompatible. Thus, the establishment of the new mode of social
control is inseparable from the realization of the principles of a *socialist
economy,* which center on a *meaningful economy of productive activity*: the

pivotal point of a rich human fulfillment in a society emancipated from the alienated and reified institutions of control.

The final point to stress is the necessarily global determination of the alternative system of social control, in confrontation with the global system of capital as a mode of control. In the world as it has been—and is still being—transformed by the immense power of capital, the social institutions constitute a closely interlocking system. Thus, there is no hope for *isolated, partial* successes—only for *global* ones—however paradoxical this might sound. Accordingly, the crucial criterion for the assessment of partial measures is whether or not they are capable of functioning as Archimedean points: i.e., as *strategic levers* for a radical restructuring of the global system of social control. This is why Marx spoke of the vital necessity of changing, from top to bottom, the conditions of existence *as a whole,* short of which all efforts directed at a socialist emancipation of mankind are doomed to failure. Such a program, it goes without saying, embraces the "micro-structures" (like the family) just as much as the most comprehensive institutions (the "macro-structures") of political and economic life. Indeed, as Marx had suggested, nothing less than a radical transformation of our whole manner of being can produce an adequate system of social control.

Its establishment will, no doubt, take time and will require the most active involvement of the whole community of producers, activating the repressed creative energies of the various social groups over matters incomparably greater in importance than deciding the color of local lamp-posts to which their power of decision-making is confined today.

The establishment of this social control will, equally, require the conscious cultivation—not in isolated individuals but in the whole community of producers, to whatever walk of life they may belong—of an uncompromising critical awareness, coupled with an intense commitment to the values of a socialist humanity, which guided the work of Isaac Deutscher to a rich fulfillment.

Thus, our memorial is not a ritual remembrance of the past but a persistent challenge to face up to the demands inherent in our own share of a shared task.

It is in this spirit that I wish to dedicate my lecture to the memory of Isaac Deutscher.

CHAPTER FOUR

Radical Politics and Transition to Socialism: Reflections on Marx's Centenary[1]

Marx wrote his *Capital* in order to help break the rule of capital under favorable conditions; that is to say, when "total social capital"—in its relentless drive to subdue everything to itself on a global scale—cannot displace any longer its contradictions and is pushed to its limits, thus foreshadowing what Marx called the "realm of the new historic form."

Today, one hundred years after Marx's death, we are a great deal closer to the conditions of capital's global breakdown and to the real possibility of that fundamental transformation, which his work was meant to identify with scientific rigor and socialist passion. Naturally, it would be rather naïve to suggest that from now on there will be no more outlets for capital's further expansion and for the displacement of many of its problems with the full involvement of the state. Equally, however, no one should doubt that we are in the midst of a crisis never experienced before on anything like a comparable scale.

Accordingly, not only are the stakes getting higher and the confrontations sharper but also the possibilities of a positive outcome are set in a new historical perspective. Precisely because the stakes are getting higher and potentially more explosive, the storehouse of compromises that formerly served so well the forces of unchallenged consensus politics is also becoming more depleted, thereby blocking certain roads and opening up some others while calling for the adoption of new strategies.

Against this background of capital's structural crisis and the concomitant new historical potentialities, it is necessary to reexamine the requirements and objective conditions of going *Beyond Capital* in the spirit of the original socialist project. For the transition to socialism on a global scale, envisaged by Marx, has acquired a new and more urgent historical actuality, today, in view of the intensity and severity of the unfolding crisis.

In this article I can address only a few, closely linked, problems. *First,* the question of what is really meant by going "beyond capital": a concept that designates the necessary objective and orienting perspective of viable socialist strategies. For the chosen *goal* necessarily conditions the stages leading to its realization, and, thus, the misidentification of the proper target of socialist transformation inevitably carries with it serious consequences for the socialist movement, as is painfully well known from past history.

The *second* problem to discuss concerns the necessity of a socialist offensive under the conditions of its new historical actuality. This implies also the necessity to face the major challenge of being compelled to embark on such an *offensive* within the framework of the existing institutions of the working class, which happened to be *defensively* constituted, under very different historical conditions, in the past.

Both going beyond capital and envisaging a socialist offensive are paradigmatic issues of a transition to socialism. They take us to the *third* problem I must briefly talk about: the need for a theory of transition, in keeping with the socioeconomic and political conditions of our own times when *objectively* the issue itself has surfaced on the historical agenda.

And *finally*—in contrast to various strategies on the left which tend to respond to the present crisis by advocating a limited "restructuring of the economy"—I wish to consider the role *radical politics* is called upon to play in that fundamental restructuring of society as a whole without which any transition to socialism is inconceivable.

1. THE MEANING OF *BEYOND CAPITAL*

As a point of departure, it is necessary to focus on the meaning of *Beyond Capital*. This happens to be an all-important problem, both theoretically and practically, with several clearly distinguishable aspects:

1.   Marx wrote *Capital* in order to help break the rule of capital. And he called his main work *Capital*, not "Capitalism," for a very good reason, as we shall see in a moment. Similarly, he defined the object of Volume One as "*Der Produktionsprozess des Kapitals*," i.e., "The Production-Process of Capital," and not as "The Process of *Capitalist* Production"—the way it has been wrongly translated into English, under Engels' supervision—which is a radically different matter.

2.   "Capital" is a dynamic *historical* category and the social force to which it corresponds appears—in the form of "monetary," "mercantile," etc. capital—many centuries before the social formation of *capitalism* as such emerges and consolidates itself. Indeed, Marx is very greatly concerned with grasping the historical specificities of the various forms of capital and their transitions into one another, until *industrial capital* becomes the dominant force of the social and economic metabolism and objectively defines the classical phase of the capitalist formation.

3.   The same is true of "commodity production," which should not be identified with *capitalist* commodity production. The former precedes the latter, again by many centuries, thus calling for a precise definition of the historical specificities of the capitalist mode of commodity production. For, as Marx insists, "commodity production necessarily turns into *capitalist* commodity production *at a certain point*."[2]

4.   The importance of (2) and (3) is not merely theoretical but more and more directly *practical* as well. For the historical dimension of capital and commodity production is not confined to the *past*, illuminating the dynamic transition from the pre-capitalist formations

to capitalism. It also asserts its necessary practical implications for the present and the future, foreshadowing the objective constraints and unavoidable structural determinants of the *post-capitalist* phase of development. Capitalism itself is not intelligible without this historical dimension of its fundamental structural characteristics, reaching back to a more or less distant past. In the same way, the real problems of a socialist transformation cannot be grasped without fully acknowledging that capital and commodity production not only *precede* but also necessarily *survive* capitalism; and they do not do so simply as a matter of "Asiatic backwardness" (which happens to be an additional complication, under determinate socio-historical and political circumstances) but as a matter of innermost structural determinations.

5.   All this has far-reaching implications for the necessary and feasible objectives of social strategies within the setting of the prevalent structural and historical determinations. Given such parameters, the socialist project, paradoxically, cannot help but to define itself in the first place in terms of a *radical disjuncture* between its *fundamental* historical objective and its *immediately* feasible one. The former aims at the establishment of a socialist society which represents a qualitatively "new historic form" (Marx) in that it succeeds in going *beyond capital* itself, thus effectively superseding the world of *capital as such*; whereas the latter is forced to define its target as attacking and overcoming the dominant forces of *capitalism* only, while necessarily remaining in a vitally important sense within the structural parameters of capital as such. By contrast, without a *radical restructuring* of capital's overall controlling framework as embedded not merely in the given economic mechanisms but in the inherited *social metabolism* in general—which is feasible only as a complex historical process, with all its contradictions and potential relapses or disruptions—it is inconceivable to bring the socialist project to its proper fruition.

Confounding (for no matter how urgent and burning a political and historical reason) the fundamental strategic objective of socialism—to go *beyond capital*—with the necessarily limited and immediately feasible objective of *negating capitalism*, and, thereafter, pretending in the name of the latter to have realized the former, produces disorientation, the loss of all objective measure, and a going around in circles, at best, in the absence of a viable measure and direction.

The real strategic objective of all socialist transformation is and remains the radical transcendence of capital itself, in its global complexity and with the totality of its given as well as potential historical configurations, and not merely this or that particular form of more or less developed (or underdeveloped) capitalism. It is possible to envisage negating and superseding *capitalism* in a particular social setting, provided that the given conditions themselves favor such historical intervention. At the same time, though, the much debated strategy of "socialism in one country" is feasible only as a limited *post-capitalist*—i.e., not yet *inherently socialist*—project. In other words, it is feasible as only one *step* in the direction of a global sociohistorical transformation whose objective cannot be other than going *beyond capital* in its entirety.

Furthermore, the unavoidable fact is that the *post-capitalist* phase as a whole remains—even if to a potentially diminishing degree—within the constraints and *objective* structural parameters of capital's ultimate determinations. The latter, contrary to Stalinist practice, should not be voluntaristically conceptualized as if they were nothing more than the *subjective*, conspiratorial manipulations of the "enemy." Consequently, the very process of radical restructuring—the crucial condition for success of the socialist project—can only make progress if the strategy aims at the radical supersession of capital *as such*, consciously and persistently reducing capital's power of regulating the social metabolism itself, instead of hailing as the realization of socialism some limited post-capitalist achievements. This can be accomplished by locating adaptable mechanisms and processes which favor the required complex transformation, in contrast to firing shots in the dark, through the adoption of more or less haphazard measures, on the basis of the false identification of the fundamental strategic aim of socialism with some immediately feasible but necessarily restricted objectives.

To put it more strongly, given the inherent character of the processes involved, various forms of post-capitalist undertaking are undoubtedly

feasible, in no matter how limited a setting, for precisely the same reason—i.e., the necessary limitation of this setting. However, they also
remain under a permanent threat. And they remain under such threat for
as long as the fundamental issue of going *beyond capital* is not settled. In
other words, this or that particular form of capitalism can be "abolished"
in a limited historical setting, but such abolition cannot provide any guarantee against its *potential revitalization or "restoration."* Everything
depends on the total configuration of the social and historical circumstances as defined by capital's more or less important role in the overall
social metabolism on a *global scale.*

2. HISTORICAL CONDITIONS
OF THE SOCIALIST OFFENSIVE

The necessity and historical actuality of the socialist offensive does not
mean the advocacy of some facile and naïvely optimistic agitational perspective—far from it. For, in the first place, the *historical* actuality of a
process of transformation—as arising from the manifold, uneven, and
conflicting determinations of an objective historical *tendency*—refers to
the *historical phase* in its *entirety*, with all its complications and potential
relapses, and not to some sudden event that produces a linear development that is without problems. It is worth recalling here Lenin's words:

> Capitalism could have been declared—and with full justice—to be "histori-
> cally obsolete" many decades ago, but that does not at all remove the need for
> a very long and very persistent struggle on the basis of capitalism.
> Parliamentarism is "historically obsolete" from the standpoint of *world histo-
> ry,* i.e., the *era* of bourgeois parliamentarism is over, and the *era* of the prole-
> tarian dictatorship has *begun.* That is incontestable. But world history is
> counted in decades.[3]

In this sense, "historical actuality" means precisely what it says: the
emergence and unfolding actualization of a trend in all of its historical
complexity, embracing a whole historical era or epoch and delimiting its
strategic parameters—for better or worse as the case might be under the

changing circumstances—and *ultimately* asserting the fundamental tendency of the epoch in question, notwithstanding all fluctuations, unevenness, and even relapses.

It cannot be stressed enough that, in the midst of the deepening *structural* crisis of capital, we may only talk about the *historical* actuality of the socialist offensive in the sense that major institutional changes are required to bring to fruition the historical tendency in question. This is because of the strongly constraining fact that the existing instruments and institutions of socialist struggle have been constituted at a qualitatively different historical conjuncture, defining themselves: (1) in opposition to *capitalism* (not to *capital* as such); and (2) in a fundamentally *defensive* way, in keeping with their essentially negating original potential and function.

Thus, the historical actuality of the socialist offensive under the new historical phase of capital's structural crisis asserts itself as: (1) the increasing difficulty and ultimate impossibility of obtaining *defensive gains*—on the model of the past—through the existing *defensive* organizations of labor. Accordingly, this means in a historical sense the end of consensus politics, carrying with it the noticeably *more aggressive posture* of the dominant forces of capital *vis-à-vis* labor; and (2) the objective pressure for radically restructuring the existing forms and institutions of socialist struggle, so as to be able to meet the new historical challenge on an organizational basis that proves itself adequate to the growing need for a strategic offensive.

What is at stake, then, is the constitution of an organizational framework capable not only of negating the ruling order but simultaneously also of exercising the vital positive functions of control, in the new form of *self-activity and self-management,* if the socialist forces are to break the vicious circle of capital's social control and their own negative and defensive dependency on it.

The historical novelty of the new situation is manifest in the qualitative redefinition of the conditions of success of even the most limited socioeconomic objectives. For in the past it was not only *possible* to obtain significant *partial gains* from capital by means of the existing defensive institutions and organizations. So much so, in fact, that the working classes of the dominant capitalist countries today have incomparably more to lose than their chains. But such gains were a necessary and positive constituent of the *inner dynamic* of *capital's self-expansion* itself (which meant, of course, that capital never had to pay a single penny for those gains).

In sharp contrast, under the new historical conditions of capital's structural crisis, even the bare maintenance of the acquired standard of living, not to mention the acquisition of meaningful additional gains, requires a major change in strategy in accordance with the historical actuality of the socialist offensive. Capital's growing *legislative attack* on the labor movement underlines the necessity of such a change in the strategic orientation of its adversary.

3. THE NEED FOR A THEORY OF TRANSITION

At the time when Marx spelled out his original conception, the accent had to be on demonstrating the inner contradictions of capital, indicating only the barest outline of what he called "the new historic form." The question of how to get from the negated world of capital to the realm of the merely "intimated" new historic form did not play any part in Marx's theoretical project. Indeed, he scorned those who engaged in such "speculations about the future."

Nor was the problem of transition relevant to Lenin prior to the October revolution. He was engaged in elaborating a strategy for "breaking the weakest link of the chain," in the hope of initiating a chain reaction which should have resulted in a problematic very different from that which actually presented itself through the painful historical constraints of an isolated Soviet revolution.

Thus, the need for a theory of transition appeared with a burning urgency, "out of the blue," in the aftermath of the October revolution and, consequently, became mixed up with the specific determinations and concerns of Soviet society. The controversy over "socialism in one country" was already a bewilderingly complex, indeed confounding, issue in that an underdeveloped and devastated country was supposed to make, in isolation and encirclement, the great leap forward on its own for the whole of humanity. But much worse was still to come. With the triumph of Stalinism in the international working-class movement, this issue had become even more confounding since the "Soviet road to socialism" had been proclaimed the compulsory model for all conceivable socialist transformation. It was uncritically adopted as a model by the adherents of the Comintern, including the major Western Communist Parties whose objective circumstances lacked the relative historical justification of "Asiatic backwardness" and encirclement for advocating such a strategy.

As a result, theorizing transition was hopelessly derailed soon after its first appearance, ending up in the blind alley of Stalinist voluntarism and various abstract negations. There were, of course, a few individual attempts that aimed at finding a way out of this blind alley—Antonio Gramsci's both humanly and theoretically heroic achievements represent their incomparable peak—but they were condemned to remain tragically isolated under the circumstances.

Nor could the openly announced intention of "de-Stalinization" produce a fundamental change in this respect. While it undoubtedly reopened the possibilities of critical self-examination (especially in the Western communist movement), the stifling of criticism in the East after a short period of "thaw"—blind to the upheavals and explosions in Germany, Poland, Hungary, Czechoslovakia, and in Poland again— underlined the severity of the crisis. It became increasingly obvious that what was really at stake was not a mere ideological factor—conceptualized in wishful and subjective categories that circularly referred to, yet never really explained even the possibility of the "personality cult," let alone provided a guarantee for its effective supersession. It was, rather, a matter of the persistent power of inertia of massive objective structures and forces, which could not be effectively dislodged except in the global strategic framework of socialist development and structural transformation.

The historical experience of Eastern Europe could not provide sufficient ground for developing both a critical and self-critical theory of transition. This was not simply due to ideological and political pressures and taboos—although, of course, they too played their part. It was primarily due to the sociohistorical limitations of the experience itself.

The urgent need for a theory of transition appeared on the historical agenda with the October revolution, but it asserted itself in an unavoidably *partial* form. This had to be the case, given the weight of the local constraints and contradictions. The revolution had to be carried on as a "holding operation" (as Lenin had called it) if it was to survive. But even more, the partiality in question was the consequence of the essentially *defensive* historical determinations to which the struggling socialist forces of the period were subjected in their unequal confrontations with capital. This defensive determination represented an overwhelming negative historical constraint, which Stalin apologetically turned into a positive virtue and model, frustrating and paralyzing even the limited dynamic potential of the international socialist movement for decades.

Today the situation is qualitatively different in that transition can no longer be conceptualized in a *limited* sense, since the need for it arises in relation to the deepening structural crisis of capital as a global phenomenon.

It is always difficult to pin down with precision the major historical demarcation lines and the beginning of a new historical phase; both because the roots of fundamental new trends reach back into the depths of past determinations, and because it takes a long time before they unfold in all their dimensions and fully assert themselves at all levels of social life. Even such gigantic historical earthquakes as 1789 and 1917—which we now count as the origin of many subsequent historical changes—are intelligible only in terms of both their roots in the past and their long, dramatic aftermath. In order to succeed in asserting their significance as seminal historical events, forbiddingly strong resistances had to be overcome.

Even if one cannot locate the beginning of the new historical phase of the necessary socialist offensive around some precise date or event, we can nevertheless identify three major social confrontations that dramatically signaled the eruption of capital's structural crisis towards the end of the 1960s:

1.   the Vietnam War and the collapse of the most openly aggressive form of American interventionism;

2.   May 1968 in France (and elsewhere, more or less at the same time, in similar social situations), clamorously demonstrating in a heartland of "advanced" capitalism the sickness of society, the fragility,

and hollowness of its loudly advertised achievements, and the striking alienation of a vast number of people from the "system"; and

3. the repression of reform attempts in Czechoslovakia and in Poland,
    underlining the growing contradictions of the societies of "actually
    existing socialism" as an *integral part of the overall structural crisis.*

Significantly, everything that happened since falls into the same three
categories, which embrace:

1. the exploitative relations of "metropolitan" or capitalistically
    advanced countries and underdeveloped ones, in their reciprocal
    determinations;

2. the problems and contradictions of the Western capitalist countries,
    taken by themselves as well as in conjunction with one another; and

3. the various post-capitalist countries or societies of "actually existing
    socialism" as related to (and at times even militarily confronting)
    one another.

Developments in the last two decades underlined, with respect to all
three dimensions, the working of some powerful forces and tendencies,
which, in their interrelatedness, define the deepening structural crisis of
capital. Let me merely list a few major events and signposts of these developments, as manifest in all three areas of our concern.

With regard to the first set of relations:

-   the end of the colonial regime in Mozambique and Angola;

-   the defeat of white racism and the transfer of power to Zimbabwe
    African National Union in Zimbabwe;

-   the collapse of the U.S. client regime run by the Colonels in
    Greece and the subsequent victory of Andreas Papandreou's
    Panhellenic Socialist Government forces;

- the disintegration of Somosa's lifelong, U.S.-backed rule in Nicaragua and the striking victory of the Sandinista Front;

- armed liberation struggles in El Salvador and elsewhere in Central America and the end of the erstwhile easy control of the region by U.S. imperialism;

- the total bankruptcy—not only figuratively but also in a literal sense—of metropolitan inspired and dominated developmental strategies all over the Third World and the eruption of massive structural contradictions in all three principal industrial powers in Latin America (Argentina, Brazil and oil-rich Mexico);

- the dramatic and total disintegration of the Shah's regime in Iran and with it a major defeat of long-established U.S. strategies in the region, calling into existence *desperately dangerous substitute strategies*—to be implemented *directly or by proxy*—ever since.

As to the second:

- the U.S. debt crisis and the growing resentment of American economic domination;

- conflicts with industrially successful Japan and increasing signs of a potentially devastating trade war;

- the eruption of major contradictions within the European Economic Community, at times to the point of threatening it with breakup;

- the failure of postwar Keynesianism and its replacement by equally unviable monetarist strategies aimed at revitalizing capital in crisis;

- massive and still growing structural unemployment and the corresponding eruption of major social disturbances on the ruins of the welfare state, following the collapse of the postwar strategy which confidently announced the realization of "full employment in a free society";

- the failure of the postwar strategy of "neo-colonialism"—with its ideology of modernization and its self-serving "transfer of technology"—and the slipping control of the advanced capitalist countries over the Third World (illustrated by the spread of debt defaults, for instance), with potentially far-reaching consequences.

And, finally, regarding the major contradictions that surfaced in the internal and external relations of the so-called societies of actually existing socialism:

- the collapse of the Chinese cultural revolution and the rapprochement between China and the West, carrying with it at times quite devastating consequences for socialist aspirations;

- the indescribable tragedy of the people of Cambodia;

- armed confrontation between China and Vietnam, and between Vietnam and Cambodia;

- Soviet occupation of Afghanistan and the ensuing armed conflict; renewed crises in Czechoslovakia;

- increasing indebtedness of several East European countries to Western bankers, to the point of bankruptcy politely and capitalistically re-baptized as "debt rescheduling";

- massive economic crisis in Poland and the emergence as well as the military repression of the grassroots Solidarity movement.

Against such a background of ubiquitous and perilously multiplying contradictions, which amount to a veritable structural crisis, it is impossible to raise the problem of transition as one of only partial significance and thus applying to no more than the specific circumstances of a historically limited conjuncture. It is no longer possible to conceive the objective of post-capitalist strategies as some kind of "holding operation," whose meaning is strictly defensive, in the hope of a significant improvement in the overall historical conditions and in the relation of forces which might later on favor the chances of a genuine socialist transformation.

The force of circumstance, tragically constraining and determining the character of a transitional effort as a holding operation, is one thing; the necessity of a radical social transformation on a global scale is quite another. Today, the need for a comprehensive theory of transition appears on the historical agenda in the perspective of the socialist offensive, on the ground of its general historical actuality, in response to the growing structural crisis of capital, which threatens the very survival of humanity.

4. RESTRUCTURING THE ECONOMY AND ITS POLITICAL PRECONDITIONS

4.1 The Dynamics of Postwar Developments

There is today a growing concern about the need for "restructuring the economy," and understandably so. The postwar years, for well over two decades, saw the unprecedented expansion and revitalization of capital—by bringing into its orbit for the first time in history the totality of global productive forces, as well as by successfully restructuring the economy so as to meet the insatiable requirements of the military-industrial complex. Now, however, the whole dynamic has come to a halt, and the system cannot any longer deliver the goods upon which its undisturbed development depends.

However, the aim of restructuring the economy appears problematic—no matter how justifiable the concern behind it. In view of the fact that the present state of affairs is the direct result of the postwar period's dramatic restructuring of capital's productive outlets, it is by no means obvious that switching resources today from some areas to others would produce the expected economic results, not to mention the overwhelming political complications involved in such an undertaking.

Considered under its principal aspects, any effort at restructuring the economy is bound to meet with great resistance. This is because the leverage with which it operates remains within the confines of capital's objective determinations and mechanisms of control, favoring itself and nothing else. To single out three main dimensions, it is not too difficult to perceive the inherent irreconcilable contradictions:

1. in the problem of productivity itself (i.e., in the ultimately self-destructive productivity of capital);

2. in the growing demands of the military-industrial complex confronting the rest of the economy;

3. in the emergence of the industrialized parts of the Third World—under the irrepressible dynamics of capital's self-expansion—as direct competitors to Western capital.

Let us briefly look at them one by one.

(1) The postwar period of development was undoubtedly fueled, above all else, by capital's ability to activate immense, formerly repressed or latent, human and material resources for its purposes of self-expansion. It significantly extended and intensified productive economic activity by increasing both the absolute size of the labor force and its relative productivity all over the world. So long as such processes of productive self-expansion could go on unhindered, there could be no problems which capital could not, in principle, overcome.

Things had to change dramatically, however, when increasing productivity itself started to conflict with the requirement of enlarging (or even just maintaining) the labor force. Under such conditions of structural unemployment, the necessary mode of functioning and the very *raison d'être* of capital are called into question as a matter of objective historical imperative, even if this is not immediately conceptualized as such by the actors involved.

Nor is it feasible to envisage a solution to this structural problem by simply "creating more jobs" through restructuring the economy. What is at stake is not really capital's *efficiency*, which might be improved by a more or less drastic reallocation of economic resources, but, on the contrary, the very nature of its *productivity*: a productivity that necessarily defines itself through the imperative of its relentless, alienated self-expansion as a *destructive productivity*, which unceremoniously demolishes everything that happens to stand in its way.

Furthermore—due to the inherently contradictory nature of capital—in periods of recession the heavily *overproduced* (and at the same time grossly *underutilized)* quantity of capital absurdly asserts itself as an extreme *scarcity of capital*, thus constraining all further productive advance and adding an *adventurist financial dimension* (as well as its quixotic counterpart, in the form of monetarism) to all the other problems. It is, therefore, impossible to see how the massive resources required for the envisaged economic restructuring could be found within the confines of capital's inner determinations, as manifest both in its devastating "productivity" and chronic "scarcity" at times of economic troubles.

(2) The second major factor of capital's dynamic postwar expansion, the staggering development of the military-industrial complex, turned equally sour, despite the state's determined efforts to extend its power or at least to keep it intact under the circumstances of hardship and cuts.

Ironically, the very fact that the problem can be formulated in this way—namely, as a call to increase or maintain military expenditure *at the expense* of social services and the economic activity that sustains them—indicates that we are facing a fundamental structural contradiction. In the past, the much-advertised technological fall-out from military developments and their claimed beneficial effects on consumer industry served as a self-evident ideological and economic justification for military waste, in addition to the military-industrial complex's ability to stimulate economic development by its huge demand on the available—and at first sight apparently limitless—material and human resources which it originally helped multiplying.

That a time might come when the multiplication of such wasteful demand cannot be sustained any longer and choices must be made between military and consumer expenditure never crossed the mind of the strategists of postwar capital-expansion. Given some inner laws and contradictions of "advanced" capital, the road opened up by the saturation-proof and self-consuming military-industrial complex had to be pursued, irrespective of the potential complications which seemed to be non-existent so long as the unhindered self-expansion of capital could be taken for granted.

The changes that occurred under these circumstances amounted, beyond any doubt, to a restructuring of the economy so powerful and encompassing in character that its intensity and impact finds no parallel in the history of capital since the industrial revolution itself. To envisage, therefore, a new restructuring of the economy by simply reversing this trend and transferring resources from the military-industrial complex to socially productive use seems to be greatly underestimating the difficulties, even in strictly economic terms. Not to mention the political and military complications involved in attempting to curtail in the required form, as well as to keep under control ever after, the might of such a powerful adversary.

(3) The industrialization of the Third World, notwithstanding its obvious subordination to the requirements and interests of Western capital, reached significant proportions in the global configuration of capital during the postwar years, especially in the last two decades.

To be sure, this industrialization was never meant to meet the needs of the starving and socially deprived people of the countries concerned, but to provide unrestrained outlets for capital-export and to generate formerly unimaginable levels of super-profit, under the ideology of modernization and the elimination of "underdevelopment." Nevertheless, due to the sheer size of the material and human resources thus activated by capital, the overall impact of such developments could not be other than phenomenal as far as the total production of profit in the global framework of capital was concerned. For despite all of the one-sided talk about "dependency," not to mention the obscenely hypocritical talk about developmental aid, Western capital had become far more dependent on the Third World—for raw materials, energy, capital-outlets, and eagerly repatriated super-profit—than the other way round.

Naturally, in this context no less than in any other, the underlying process can only be characterized as capital's leapfrogging from one con-

tradiction to another, in keeping with the insoluble contradictoriness of
its innermost nature. Capital derives its original dynamic from the inner
determination of its nature to overcome encountered obstacles, however
great, *displacing* at the same time some major contradictions. But it does
this only to end up with the *regeneration of its contradictions with a
vengeance,* on an incomparably larger scale than that which had brought
it into being in the first place.

Accordingly, no matter how bastardized and cynically manipulated
the neo-capitalist industrialization of the Third World had to be in its
inception and execution, inevitably it also acquired its own dynamics and
local momentum, leading to an ultimately irreconcilable contradiction
between the *local dynamics* and the original *metropolitan intent.* This
took the form of establishing powerful production units whose very existence enhances the prospects of an uncontrollable trade war, in addition
to causing the structural bankruptcy and closedown of entire branches of
labor-intensive industries in the advanced mother countries, in the explo-
sively contradictory—unemployment generating—overall interest of
Western expatriate capital.

This is not the place to enter into the details of such developments.
However, it must be emphasized in the present context that the competitive complications arising out of this dynamic, with their potentially
destructive repercussions on the core of advanced capital, do not represent by any means the sum total of the difficulties and contradictions of
these sets of relations. We must add to them the growing internal contradictions of the developing economies themselves: the by now all too obvious collapse of the much advertised "developmental strategies" and the
corresponding halt of the originally spectacular local rates of expansion
(as in Brazil and Mexico, for instance).

All these factors cannot but underline the insuperable difficulties facing any effort aimed at restructuring the economy, as they present themselves under this crucial dimension of global capital. For the problem of
restructuring cannot be considered other than a comprehensive one, in
every sense of the word. This is because in the contemporary world we
are confronted with a bewilderingly complex and contradictory network
of *reciprocal dependencies* on a global scale, with multiplying and ever-
intensifying troubles and demands in every particular area, by now well

beyond the control of any single center, no matter how powerful and "advanced."

4.2 Alternatives to the Dominant Economic Imperatives

Thus—viewed in relation to its main internal and international dimensions—the question of restructuring the economy defines itself as:

1. The necessity of generating a *new type of productivity* on the ruins of capital's wasteful and destructive subordination of the productive forces and energies of society to its own perverse need for self-expansion. This requirement also implies generating an adequately expandable supply of funds and resources, in harmony with the new type of productivity; instead of one that constrains and potentially cripples it, since the absurd overproduction and scarcity of capital today necessarily straitjackets the given mode of productivity.

2. The challenge of instituting a viable alternative to the military-industrial complex. This presents itself as:

   (a) the necessity of finding an economic solution to the most destructive law of capital which brought it into being in the first place—the *decreasing rate of utilization*, tending towards the zero rate; and

   (b) the creation of the political conditions for collective security and world disarmament, parallel to the establishment of a new institutional framework of inter-State relations under which the military-industrial complex loses its self-serving justification and legitimacy.

3. The institution of a radically new and truly equitable relationship with the Third World on the basis of a positive recognition of the reciprocal dependencies and necessary interdeterminations in a world whose social and economic constituents can no longer be kept either isolated from or structurally subordinated to one another if we are to see a sustainable global development. A problem which, not surprisingly, efforts like the Brandt Commission's Report do not even

scratch the surface of (not to mention the derision with which they are greeted and swept aside by the governing establishment to which their authors themselves once belonged). Yet, here we have to face a problem of the greatest importance, which, sadly and rather less understandably, Western socialists dedicate far too little attention.

Considered in these terms, the task of restructuring the economy turns out to be primarily *political* and *social*, and not *economic*.

To be sure, all sociopolitical objectives have their necessary *economic implications*: restructuring the economy without a major economic intervention at the appropriate level would represent a very odd exception. However, things are decidedly not the other way round—i.e., we are not facing a primarily economic challenge, with some more or less serious *political implications*, as it is often conceptualized—when the issue is: how to break the vicious circle of capital's "iron determinations" to which no known economic mechanism can provide an answer.

If, therefore, "restructuring the economy" is meant to equal "restructuring society" as a whole—"from top to bottom," as Marx once suggested—there can be no disagreement with that aim.[4] But it cannot be stressed enough that the resistances and obstacles to be overcome in the course of realizing such an aim are bound to remain primarily political and social for the entire historical period of transition whose objective is to go *beyond capital,* in order to create the social and economic structures of the new historic form.

Times of major economic crises always open up a sizeable breach in the established order, which no longer succeeds in delivering the goods that served as its unquestionable justification. Such breaches may be enlarged, in the service of social restructuring, or filled in for shorter or longer duration, in the interest of capital's continued survival, depending on the general historical circumstances and on the relation of forces in the political and social arena. Given the temporal dimension of the problem— i.e., the relatively long timescale for producing significant economic results, under the extreme urgency of the crisis—only a radical *political* initiative can move into the breach: a fact that greatly enhances the power of political action under such conditions. (Theories which exaggerate the "autonomy" of politics—to the point of unrealistically predicating or implying its effective *independence*—tend to generalize characteristics valid for the initial phase of a major crisis, but not under normal circumstances.)

The *immediate* manifestations of the crisis are *economic*—from inflation to unemployment, and from the bankruptcy of local industrial and commercial enterprises to a general trade-war and the potential collapse of the international financial system. As such, the pressure emanating from the given social base inevitably tends to define the task at hand in terms of finding urgent *economic* answers at the level of the crises-manifestations themselves while leaving their *social causes* intact.

An economic definition of what *needs* to be done as well as what *can* be done under the circumstances of the acknowledged "economic emergency" takes shape—from "tightening the belt" and "accepting the necessary sacrifices" to "creating real jobs," "injecting new investment funds," and "increasing productivity and competitiveness." All of this imposes the *social premises* of the established order (in the name of purely *economic* imperatives) on the socialist political initiative potentially favored by the crisis, prior to its unwitting adoption of capital's social and economic horizon. As a result, the restructuring potential of revolutionary politics is nullified: it is dissipated in the course of struggling with narrowly defined economic tasks—invariably at the expense of its own supporters—within the framework of the old social premises and structural determinations. Thereby, as a matter of bitter irony, a revitalization of capital is engendered, contradicting the original intentions.

4.3 The Historical Moment of Radical Politics

The difficulty is that the "moment" of radical politics is strictly limited by the nature of the crises in question and the temporal determinations of their unfolding. The breach opened up at times of crisis cannot be left open forever, and the measures adopted to fill it, from the earliest steps onwards, have their own logic and cumulative impact on subsequent interventions. Furthermore, both the existing socioeconomic structures and their corresponding framework of political institutions tend to act against radical initiatives by their very inertia, as soon as the worst moment of the crisis is over. Thus, it becomes possible to contemplate again *the line of least resistance*. And no one can consider radical restructuring as the line of least resistance since, by its very nature, it necessarily involves upheaval and the disconcerting prospect of the unknown.

No immediate economic achievement can offer a way out of this dilemma so as to prolong the lifespan of revolutionary politics. This is because such limited economic achievements—made within the confines of the old premises—act in the opposite direction by relieving the most pressing crisis symptoms and, as a result, reinforcing the old reproductive mechanism shaken by the crisis.

As history amply testifies, at the first sign of "recovery," politics is pushed back into its traditional role of helping to sustain and enforce the given socioeconomic determinations. The claimed recovery itself, reached on the basis of "well-tried economic motivations," acts as the self-evident ideological justification for reverting to the subservient and routine role of politics in harmony with the dominant institutional framework. Thus, radical politics can only accelerate its own demise (and thereby shorten, instead of extending as it should, the favorable moment of major political intervention) if it consents to define its own scope in terms of limited economic targets which are in fact necessarily dictated by the established socioeconomic structure in crisis.

Paradoxical as it may sound, only a radical self-determination of politics can prolong the moment of radical politics. If that moment is not to be dissipated under the weight of immediate economic pressures, a way must be found to extend its influence well beyond the peak of the crisis itself (the peak, that is, when radical politics tends to assert its effectiveness as a rule). The temporal duration of the crisis as such cannot be prolonged at will—nor should it be, since voluntarist politics, with its artificially manipulated "state of emergency," may only attempt to do so at its own peril, thereby alienating the masses of the people instead of securing their support. As such, the solution can only arise from successfully turning *fleeting time* into *enduring space* by means of restructuring the powers and institutions of decision-making.

To put it in another way, radical politics is only *temporarily* favored by the crisis, which can just as easily turn against it beyond a certain point. That is to say, beyond the point when either its economic success revitalizes capital, or its failure to deliver the anticipated economic improvement dramatically undermines its own mandate and claim to legitimacy.

Thus, to succeed in its original aim, radical politics must transfer at the height of the crisis its aspirations—in the form of effective *powers of decision-making* at all levels and in all areas, including the economy—to the social body itself from which subsequent material and political demands would emanate. This is the only way in which radical politics could sustain its own line of strategy.

Such transfer of political power, together with its embedding into the socio-economic structure itself, is only feasible at times of major structural crises: when, that is, the traditional premises of the dominant social and economic metabolism not only *can* but also *must* be questioned.

Given the existing social division of labor, this questioning in the first place cannot arise anywhere else but in the "political arena properly so called" (Marx). If, however, the questioning remains trapped within the confines of the strictly institutional forms of political action, it is bound to be defeated by the necessary reemergence of past economic, political, and institutional inertia.

The alternative to being trapped in this way is to use the critical and liberating potentials inherent in the historically favorable moment of socialist politics to turn its radical aims into an enduring dimension of the social body as a whole and to do this by asserting and diffusing its own transient power through an effective *transfer of power* to the sphere of *mass self-activity.*

The failure to consciously pursue such a course of action can only turn defeat from a more or less real possibility into a self-imposed certainty. This is why the aim of restructuring the economy badly needs qualifications. In our present context, its inner truth reveals itself as the need for a *radical restructuring of politics itself* through which the realization of socialist economic aims first becomes feasible at all. (Hence, the urgency of complementing parliamentary and institutionalized politics by growing areas and forms of *extra-parliamentary action.)*

The socialist offensive cannot be carried to its positive conclusion unless radical politics succeeds in *prolonging its moment,* so as to be able to implement the policies required by the magnitude of its tasks. The only way, however, in which the historical moment of radical politics can be prolonged and extended—without, that is, resorting to dictatorial solutions—is to *fuse* the power of political decision-making with the social base from which it has been alienated for so long.

To achieve this end requires creating a new mode of political action and a new structure of genuinely mass-oriented and determined social, economic, and political interchanges. This is why a truly socialist restructuring of the economy can only proceed in the closest conjunction with a *mass-oriented restructuring of politics* as its necessary precondition.

CHAPTER FIVE

Bolívar and Chávez:
The Spirit of Radical Determination[1]

1. FEATHERS CARRIED BY THE TEMPEST

In the Summer of 2005, Venezuela commemorated the bicentenary of Simón Bolívar's oath, made in the presence of his great teacher, Simón Rodríguez—a man who later in Paris, well before Marx, frequented socialist secret societies and returned to South America only in 1823. Bolívar's oath took place on August 15, 1805, on the outskirts of Rome. Already the place itself—the hill of Monte Sacro—which they had chosen together for this solemn occasion, was indicative of the nature of the young Bolívar's historical pledge. On the hill of Monte Sacro, twenty-three centuries earlier, the rebellious protest of the plebeians against the patricians in Ancient Rome, under the leadership of Sicinio, was supposed to have taken place. At that time the rebellion of the Roman populace is said to have been brought to an end by the rhetoric of that notorious pillar of the established order, Senator Menenius Agrippa, who was preaching the familiar wisdom of the ruling classes according to which the people "not destined to rule" should willingly accept "*their place* in the *natural order* of society."

In firm defiance of the resignation that emanates from the successfully imposed iniquitous relations of power everywhere, the young Bolívar expressed his determination on Monte Sacro to dedicate his life to a struggle envisaging a victorious outcome against colonial domination in his part of the world. These were his words:

> I swear before you; I swear by the god of my fathers; I swear by my ancestors; I swear by my honor and I swear by my homeland that I will not allow my arm to rest, nor my soul to repose, until we have broken the chains which oppress us by the will of Spanish power.[2]

Bolívar never wavered in his radical determination as expressed in his oath, not even under the most adverse circumstances. The years ahead made him realize that fundamental changes had to be made not only in the international political and military power relations but, more profoundly, in the existing social order if the project of putting an end to colonial rule was to succeed. Such radical social changes included the liberation of the slaves, which his own class vehemently opposed. Even his beloved sister considered him "crazy," because of his unyielding insistence on *equality*.

Bolívar called equality *"the law of laws,"* adding that "without equality all freedoms, all rights perish. For it we must make sacrifices."[3] He professed all of this in a truly uncompromising sense. He proved the validity of his own deeply held principles and beliefs, and did not hesitate for a moment to free all of the slaves on his own estates, in his resolve to give as broad a social base as possible to the struggle for a complete and irreversible emancipation from deeply entrenched colonial rule. In his magnificent address to the Congress of Angostura, in February 1819, he singled out the liberation of the slaves as the most vital of all of his own orders and decrees:

> I leave it to your sovereign decision to reform or revoke all of the statutes and decrees enacted by me; but I plead with you to confirm the *absolute liberty of the slaves,* as I would plead for my life and for the life of the Republic.[4]

He did this several decades before the vital human issue of the emancipation of the slaves was raised and partially settled in North America. For the Founding Fathers of the United States never had half a concern in their minds, and even less in their hearts, for putting an end to the inhumane system of slavery of which they were themselves direct beneficiaries. The terrible legacy of this fateful omission has continued to assert itself in different forms for centuries, manifesting in a most tragic way even in our own days, as witnessed in New Orleans at the time of Hurricane Katrina.

As a necessary counterweight to both the "Holy Alliance," which included Spain, and, even more importantly, the growing imperial ambitions of the United States of America, Bolívar tried to constitute a lasting Confederation of the Latin American nations. Not surprisingly, however, his efforts directed toward that end were not only frustrated but also totally nullified by the ever-more-powerful United States and its allies.

Showing great insight into the prevailing trend of historical development, reaching down to our own times, Bolívar was in the end forced to conclude that *"the United States of North America seem to be destined by providence to condemn America to misery in the name of Liberty."*[5] As we all know, George W. Bush's speeches—irrespective of who writes them— are peppered with the unctuous recitation of the word "liberty." All that has changed since Simón Bolívar's days is that today the United States of America claims to be destined by divine providence to treat as it pleases, "in the name of Liberty," not only South America but the entire world, employing even the most violent military aggression against those who dare to oppose its global imperial design.

Even the Anglican Bishops rejected, in a document rendered public on September 19, 2005, such presumption of righteousness and providential destiny as the orienting principle of U.S. foreign policy, although they—understandably but wrongly—attributed it to the influence of Fundamentalist Christianity. Understandably, because on that basis they could utter *ex officio* an authoritative condemnation of a "theologically misconceived" position. But wrongly, because this foreign policy orientation of the U.S. ruling classes goes back in history all the way to Simón Bolívar's days, if not earlier. And those who like to ascribe it simply to George W. Bush's administration would be well advised to remember that it was a Democratic President, Bill Clinton, who arrogantly declared while holding office—in full unison with his government, from Secretary of State Madeleine Albright to Labor Secretary Robert B. Reich—that there is *"only one necessary nation: the United States of America."*[6] On that count, as proclaimed by no less a figure than the twice-elected Clinton, the other nations should be condemned by the "one and only necessary nation" for their totally unacceptable aspirations to sovereign decision-making, without the slightest concern for democracy and liberty, implying that they were guilty of *"ethnic pandaemonium,"* to use the phrase of Democratic Senator Daniel Patrick Moynihan.[7]

Bolívar considered legal equality, the "law of laws," absolutely indispensable for the constitution of a society that would prove politically sustainable against the powers that internally tended to disrupt its potential development and tried to violate and even to nullify its sovereignty in its international relations. He insisted that "physical inequality" must be counteracted, unfailingly, under all circumstances because it is an "injustice of nature." And he was realistic enough to admit that legal equality could not do the job of correcting physical inequality beyond a certain extent and in a limited way.[8] Not even when the legal measures introduced by the legislators were of a fundamental social significance, as indeed his liberation of the slaves happened to be.

What was necessarily required in order to make the given social order truly viable was the transformation of the whole fabric of society far beyond even such measures as the legal emancipation of the slaves. Not surprisingly, therefore, in his groping towards the required solutions for which the historical time had not yet arrived, Bolívar encountered great hostility even in the Latin American countries to which he rendered an unequalled service, acknowledged by the unique title of *El Libertador* which he had been honored with at the time. Thus, outrageous as it must sound to us today, he had to spend his final days in tragic isolation.

As to his adversaries in the United States of America, who felt threatened by the spread of his enlightened conception of equality—both internally and in the conduct of inter-state relations—they did not hesitate to condemn and dismiss him as *"the dangerous madman of the South."*[9]

With a great *sense of proportion*—a virtue absolutely vital for everyone, and especially for all major political figures who have the privilege, in our societies, of making decisions which deeply affect the life of countless people—Bolívar said about himself that he was *"a feather carried by the tempest.*" This kind of assessment of one's role in society could not be more alien to the apologists of the established social and political order who would like to render any significant institutional change impossible, whether it is brought about by social tempests or even by slow degrees, despite the lip service paid at times to the latter. Moreover, such people are invariably engaged in the futile task of trying to *undo* the changes that have already asserted themselves in the course of historical development. Thus, they continue to deny that there can be deep-seated real *causes* behind the erupting social and political tempests which carry on their wings, as Bolivarian "feathers," the political figures who insist with radical passion on the necessity of fundamental social changes. And when our incurable apologists cannot altogether close their eyes to the fact of the periodic eruption of social tempests, they prefer to conveniently attribute them to *"irrationality,"* to the "acceptance by the mob of *mindless populism,"* and the like, thereby pretending to give a rational answer to the challenge they are supposed to face while in fact running away from the problem itself. They have to do that because they have absolutely no sense of proportion; nor could they ever acquire it.

In this spirit, the broadly distributed weekly, the London *Economist* refuses to give any meaning at all to the expression "Bolivarian Revolution," despite the fact that the political leadership of Venezuela, in conjunction with its consistent references to the unfinished project of Simón Bolívar's age, is engaged in setting in motion a far-reaching transformation of the country. Indeed, a transformation which continues to reverberate across the continent and generate significant rejoinders in other parts of Latin America. With a deliberately insulting intent *The Economist* puts always in sarcastic inverted commas the word "Bolivarian"—as if anything Bolivarian should be considered self-evidently absurd—in place of seriously addressing the issues themselves, which it wishfully tries to dismiss without any argument. The inverted commas are supposed to do the job of refutation, in the form of an aprioristic disqualification of the ongoing developments in South America. In this peculiar fashion, they pretend to provide an irrefutable proof. However, the only thing the editors of *The Economist* can prove by the painfully repetitive use of sarcastic inverted commas is their own venomous mindlessness. Being totally subservient to the interests of the U.S.

ruling circles, as the self-appointed propagandists of the annual economic summit held in Davos, they seem to think even today that Bolívar was
nothing more than a *"dangerous madman of the South."* In this way also
they characterize and peremptorily dismiss those who are determined to
bring his project up-to-date.

The truth of the matter is that lasting radical achievements can only
be built—*cumulatively* and in a consciously sustained way—on the meaningful appropriation of the progressive tradition which preceded ongoing
efforts and points in the same direction, despite all adversity. Neither the
nature of what can be really built upon, and thereby positively appropri-
ated, nor the long-term overall direction of humanity's historical development itself can be chosen arbitrarily. Our social universe is overburdened
with immense problems, both regarding the ever-intensifying explosive
inequalities inherited from the past and the increasingly untenable
encroachment of capital's mode of social metabolic reproduction on
nature, which threatens us with ecological disaster. These are the reasons
why the conservative and reactionary attempts to *reverse* the direction of
historical time are in the end condemned to failure. They are *structurally
incapable* of producing cumulative achievements, whatever the successes
which they can temporarily impose on society—due to the prevailing but
ever more *unstable* relations of power which bring more and more repressive forms of control to the fore even in formerly democratic countries—
at the cost of great suffering inflicted upon hundreds of millions of people. Neither evasion nor intensified repression can do their intended job
indefinitely. For both are *prodigally and catastrophically wasteful* in the
long run. The tremendous problems of our social universe must be confronted sooner or later in their *substantive* dimensions, as opposed to the
formal camouflage of democracy and liberty, which we are all too familiar
with.

As we know only too well, the historical tempest, which carries feathers like Simón Bolívar, can temporarily die down without fulfilling its
original promise. The objectives set by even the most distinguished historical figures can be realized only when their time truly arrives both in an
objective and in a subjective sense. Despite his tragic isolation in the end,
Bolívar's contribution to solving some of the greatest challenges of his
time, and in a well identifiable sense also of ours, is monumental. So too

is the contribution of José Martí in Cuba who followed in his footsteps. We cannot succeed without consciously building on the legacy they have bequeathed to us as a task for the future, redefined in the present in accordance with prevailing circumstances. In his appeals to the people, Bolívar had put into relief his conviction that: "The day of America has arrived and no human power can delay nature's course guided by the hand of Providence."[10] Toward the end of his life, he was forced to concede that, tragically, the day of America, as he had envisaged it before, had not yet arrived.

The principal impediment in this respect was the sharp contrast between the political unity of the Latin American countries advocated by Bolívar and the deeply adversarial and conflictual constituents of their social microcosms. Given the fact that their social microcosms were torn by internal antagonisms, even the noblest and most eloquent appeals to political unity could work only while the menace presented by the Spanish colonial adversary was acute. But by itself such a menace could not remedy the internal contradictions of the given social microcosms. Nor could the situation be radically altered by Bolívar's far-sighted identification of the danger quoted above. Namely, that "the United States of North America seem to be destined by providence to condemn America to misery in the name of Liberty," a danger even more strongly underlined, in the same spirit, by José Martí sixty years later.[11] Both men were as realistic in their diagnoses of dangers as they were generous in advocating an ideal solution to humanity's grave problems. Bolívar proposed bringing all nations of humanity harmoniously together with the Isthmus of Panama made the capital of our globe, in the same way "as Constantine wanted to make Byzantium the capital of the antique hemisphere."[12] And Martí insisted that *patria es humanidad*: humanity is our homeland.

But when these ideals were formulated, historical time still pointed in the opposite direction: towards the frightful intensification of the social antagonisms and the horrendous bloodletting of two world wars arising from those antagonisms. Moreover, the concomitant threat in our days is even greater than ever before. Indeed, it is *qualitatively* greater because today nothing less than the very survival of humanity is at stake. Naturally, that does not make the long advocated ideals themselves obsolete. Quite the contrary, it can only underline their growing urgency. Nevertheless, it remains as true today as it was in Bolívar's time that one cannot envisage the sustainable functioning of humanity's social *macrocosm* without overcoming the internal antagonisms of its *microcosms:* the adversarial and conflictual constitutive cells of our society under capital's mode of social metabolic control. For a cohesive and socially viable macrocosm is conceivable only on the basis of the corresponding and humanly rewarding constitutive cells of interpersonal relations.

Today, the historical circumstances are fundamentally different from the time of Bolívar's triumphs and ultimate tragic defeat. They are different in that the intervening sociohistorical development has put on the agenda the realization of the once denied objectives in a twofold sense. First, by opening up the *possibility* of instituting a potentially harmonious macrocosm on a *global* scale, beyond the devastating conflicts of past inter-state confrontations which had to culminate in the ravages of imperialism. It is this possibility which the World Social Forum is trying to stress in its recurrent appeal: *"Another world is possible."* The second aspect of the same proposition is inseparable from the first, removing the vagueness of all talk confined to *possibility* alone. If the possibility in question does not indicate a degree of *probability and necessity,* it cannot mean anything at all. In our present context the advocated cohesive and globally sustainable social macrocosm—in sharp contrast to all wishfully promoted but unrealizable capitalist propaganda about neoliberal "globalization"—is inconceivable without theoretically defining and practically articulating the constitutive cells of social interchange in a *genuine socialist way*.

This is how *possibility* and *necessity* are combined in a dialectical unity in our present day, historically specific, social universe. *Possibility,* because without overcoming the structural determinations of capital's irreconcilable antagonisms—for which the socialist project had arisen in the course of humanity's historical development—it is quite futile even to dream about instituting a globally sustainable social universe. And *necessity*—not some kind of mechanistic fatality but a literally vital and irrepressible need—because the annihilation of humankind is our destiny if in the course of the coming few decades we do not succeed in *totally eradicating capital* from our established mode of social metabolic reproduction. The principal lesson of the Soviet implosion is that we can only expect capitalist restoration if defining socialism in terms of the overthrow of the capitalist state is substituted for the much more fundamental and difficult task of eradicating capital from our entire social order.

It is quite impossible to be engaged today in the great historic task of capital's eradication, positively oriented toward a sustainable future, without activating the full resources of the spirit of *radical determination,* in tune with the requirements of our age. Bolívar did this the best way he could under the circumstances of his own time. It is true that the time has actually arrived for the realization of the Bolívarian objectives in their broadest perspective, as President Chávez has been advocating them for some time. This is why capital's propagandists, who use the term *Bolívarian project* satirically, can only make fools of themselves. *Historical continuity* does not mean mechanical repetition but *creative renewal* in the deepest sense of the term. Thus, saying that the time has arrived for the realization of the Bolívarian objectives—brought up to date for our own historical conditions, with all their intensifying urgency and clearly identifiable significance for the rest of the world—means precisely that a *socialist* sense must be given to radical transformations, if we really care about instituting them. The major speeches and interviews of President Chávez—in which he puts into relief the dramatic alternative of *"socialism or barbarism"*—make all of this very clear today.[13]

The task of radical renewal is by no means confined to Latin America. The social and political movements of the European Left, as well as of North America, are also in need of a major reassessment of their past and present strategies, in view of their painful defeats in the last few decades. The clearly identifiable social and political ferment in Latin America, going back to the time of the Cuban Revolution and manifest for decades in many different parts of that continent, not least in Venezuela, has much to say about the fundamental question of "what is to be done?" Precisely for that reason we must open our eyes to and express our solidarity with the creative renewal of the Bolívarian tradition in Venezuela in the last two decades.

Unfortunately, far too little is known about the recent past of this movement outside Latin America, despite the direct relevance of some of its main tenets for all of us. Thus, before turning to the question of our present-day prospects of development, in the final section of this chapter, I present in the next section what I wrote in 1993 on the Bolívarian project, five years before the watershed Presidential elections in Venezuela.[14]

2. CHÁVEZ'S RADICAL CRITIQUE
OF POLITICS IN 1993

The critique of the parliamentary system from a radical perspective did not begin with Marx. We find it powerfully expressed already in the eighteenth century in Rousseau's writings. Starting from the position that sovereignty belongs to the people and cannot be rightfully alienated, Rousseau argued that for the same reasons it cannot be legitimately turned into any form of representational abdication:

> The deputies of the people, therefore, are not and cannot be its representatives; they are merely its stewards, and can carry through no definitive acts. Every law the people has not ratified in person is null and void—is, in fact, not a law. The people of England regards itself as free; but it is grossly mistaken; it is free only during the election of members of parliament. As soon as they are elected, slavery overtakes it, and it is nothing. The use it makes of the short moments of liberty it enjoys shows indeed that it deserves to lose them.[15]

Rousseau also made the important point that, although the power of legislation cannot be divorced from the people even through parliamentary representation, the executive functions must be considered in a very different light. As he had put it:

> In the exercise of the legislative power, the people cannot be represented; but in that of the executive power, which is only the force that is applied to give the law effect, it both can and should be represented.[16]

Rousseau has been systematically misrepresented and abused by "democratic" ideologues, even those of the socialist jet-set, because he insisted that *"liberty cannot exist without equality,"* [17] which, therefore, rules out even the most feasible form of representation as necessarily discriminatory and iniquitous hierarchy. However, as we can see here, Rousseau put forward a much more practicable exercise of political and administrative power than what he is usually credited with or indeed is accused of doing. Significantly, in this process of tendentious misrepresentation, both of the vitally important principles of Rousseau's theory, usable in a suitably adapted form also by socialists, have been disqualified and thrown overboard. The truth of the matter is that the power of fundamental decision-making should never be divorced from the popular masses. The veritable horror story of the Soviet system, run against the people by the Stalinist bureaucracy in the name of socialism, conclusively demonstrated this. At the same time, however, the fulfillment of specific administrative and executive functions in all domains of the social reproductive process can indeed be *delegated* to members of the given community, provided that it is done under rules autonomously set by and properly controlled, at all stages of the substantive decision-making process, by the associated producers.

Thus, the difficulties do not reside in the two basic principles themselves, as formulated by Rousseau, but in the way in which they must be related to capital's material and political control of the social metabolic process. The establishment of a socialist form of decision-making—in accordance with the principles of both inalienable rule-determining power (i.e., the sovereignty of labor not as a particular class but as the universal condition of society) and delegating specific roles and functions under well-defined, flexibly distributed, and appropriately supervised, rules—would require entering and radically restructuring capital's antagonistic material domains. This is a process which would have to go well beyond what could be successfully regulated by considerations derived from Rousseau's principle of inalienable popular sovereignty and its delegatory corollary. In other words, in a socialist order the legislative process would have to be fused with the production process itself in such a way that the necessary *horizontal division of labor* should be complemented by a system of self-determined *coordination* of labor, from the local to the global levels.

This relationship is in sharp contrast to capital's pernicious *vertical division of labor*, which is complemented by the "separation of powers" in an alienated, and on the laboring masses unalterably superimposed, "democratic political system." For the vertical division of labor under the rule of capital necessarily affects and incurably infects every facet also of the horizontal division of labor, from the simplest productive functions to the most complicated balancing processes of the legislative jungle. The latter is an ever denser legislative jungle; its endlessly multiplying rules and institutional constituents must play their vital part in keeping firmly under control the actually or potentially challenging behavior of labor, watchful over limited labor disputes and safeguarding capital's overall rule in society at large. Also, it must somehow reconcile at any particular temporal slice of the unfolding historical process—to the extent to which such reconciliation is feasible at all—the separate inter-ests of the plurality of capitals with the uncontrollable dynamics of the totality of social capital tending towards its ultimate self-assertion as a global entity.

In a recent rejoinder to Rousseau's critique of parliamentary repre-sentation, Hugo Chávez Frias, the leader of a radical movement in Venezuela—the *Movimiento Bolívariano Revolucionário* [MBR-200, marking the 200th anniversary of Bolívar's birth]—writes in response to the chronic crisis of his country's sociopolitical system:

> With the appearance of the populist parties the suffrage was converted into a tool for putting to sleep in order to enslave the Venezuelan people in the name of democracy. For decades the populist parties based their discourse on innumerable paternalistic promises devised to melt away popular conscious-ness. The alienating political lies painted the promised land to be reached via a rose garden. The only thing the Venezuelans had to do was to go to the elec-toral urns, and hope that everything will be solved without the minimal pop-ular effort. . . . Thus the act of voting was transformed into the beginning and the end of democracy.[18]

The author of these lines stands the second highest in popular esteem in Venezuela (second only to Rafael Caldera) among all public figures, embracing all walks of life. Thus, he could easily win high public office if he so desired, which refutes the usual argument that people who criticize the existing political system only do so because they are unable to meet the arduous requirements of democratic elections. As a matter of fact, Hugo Chávez at the time of writing (in 1993) rejects the siren song of political opinion formers—who try to pacify people by saying that there is no need to worry about the crisis because there is "only a little time" to go to the new elections—for very different reasons. He points out that, although usual political wisdom calls for "a little more patience," "every minute hundreds of children are born in Venezuela whose health is endangered for lack of food and medicine, while billions are stolen from the national wealth, and in the end what remains of the country is bled dry. There is no reason why one should give any credence to a political class which demonstrated towards society that it has no will at all to institute change."[19] For this reason Chávez counterposes to the existing system of parliamentary representation the idea that: "The sovereign people must transform itself into the object *and the subject* of power. This option is not negotiable for revolutionaries."[20]

As to the institutional framework in which this principle should be realized, he projects that in the course of radical change:

> Federal state electoral power will become the political-juridical component through which the citizens will be depositories of popular sovereignty whose exercise will thereafter really remain in the hands of the people. Electoral power will be extended over the entire sociopolitical system of the nation, establishing the channels for a veritable polycentric distribution of power, displacing power from the centre towards the periphery, increasing the effective power of decision making and the autonomy of the particular communities and municipalities. The Electoral Assemblies of each municipality and state will elect Electoral Councils which will possess a permanent character and will function in absolute independence from the political parties. They will be able to establish and direct the most diverse mechanisms of Direct Democracy: popular assemblies, referenda, plebiscites, popular initiatives, vetoes, revocation, etc. . . . Thus the concept of *participatory* democracy will be changed into a form in which democracy based on popular sovereignty constitutes itself as the *protagonist* of power. It is precisely at such borders that we must draw the limits of advance of Bolivarian democracy. Then we shall be very near to the territory of *utopia*.[21]

Whether such ideas can be turned into reality or remain utopian ideals cannot be decided within the confines of the political sphere. The latter is itself in need of the type of radical transformation that foreshadows from the outset the perspective of the "withering away of the state."

In Venezuela, as much as *90 percent of the population* demonstrates its "rebellion against the absurdity of the vote through its electoral abstention."[22] Traditional political practices and the apologetic and legitimating use to which the "democratic electoral system" is put falsely claim for the system the unchallengeable justification of a "mandate conferred by the majority." As such, no condemnation of vacuous parliamentary paternalism can be considered too sharp. Nor can it be seriously argued that high electoral participation is itself proof of actually existing democratic popular consensus. After all, in some Western democracies the act of voting is compulsory and may in fact add up in its legitimating value to no more than the most extreme forms of openly critical or pessimistically resigned abstentionism. Nevertheless, the measure of validity for subjecting the parliamentary representational system to the necessary radical critique is the strategic undertaking to exercise the "sovereignty of labor"—not only in political assemblies, no matter how *direct* they might be with regard to their organization and mode of political decision-making, but also in the self-determined productive and distributive life-activity of the social individuals in every single domain and at all levels of the social metabolic process.

This is what draws the line of demarcation between the socialist revolution which is socialist in its *intent*—like the October Revolution of 1917—and the "*permanent revolution*" of effective socialist transformation. For without the progressive and ultimately complete transfer of material reproductive and distributive decision-making to the associated producers there can be no hope of the members of the post-revolutionary community transforming themselves into the *subject* of power.

3. PROSPECTS FOR DEVELOPMENT

As we can see from the quotations taken from *Pueblo, Sufragio y Democracia*, in the previous section, the continuity in calling for a sustainable socialist transformation in our day, in the spirit of radical determination, is most remarkable. This is rightly so. After so much struggle and so many sacrifices devoted, all over the world, across centuries, to the cause of human emancipation, it is even more emphatically true today than ever before—in the midst of the deepening structural crisis of the capital system which threatens our very survival—that: "The sovereign people must transform itself into the object *and the subject* of power. This option is *not negotiable* for revolutionaries." A truth firmly stressed in his 1993 pamphlet by Hugo Chávez Frias, five years before his election to the Presidency.

Without such transformation, in the deepest and most enduring sense of the term—which means nothing less than the necessity to acquire *conscious control* over their conditions of existence by the social individuals— the old order of hierarchical domination is bound to reassert itself, even against the best intentions of radical change. This is what puts on the historical agenda, with undeniable urgency, the question of socialism in the twenty-first century. A form of socialism in which—and through which— the people can not only *become* but also *remain* the sovereign subject of power in every domain. Only in that way is it possible to successfully face up to the immense challenges and ever-increasing dangers of our time. Definitely, there can be no other way.

The social and intellectual ferment in Latin America promises more for the future, in this respect, than what we can find for the time being in capitalistically advanced countries. This is understandably so, because the need for a truly radical change is that much more pressing in Latin America than in Europe and the United States. "Modernization" and "development" proved to be empty promises, and for the people at the receiving end of the policies a complete failure. It remains true that socialism, as an alternative social reproductive order, must qualify as a universally viable approach, embracing also the most developed capitalist areas of the world, including the United States. However, we cannot think of this problem in terms of a time sequence in which a future social revolution in the capitalistically advanced countries must take precedence over the possibility of radical change everywhere else. Given the massive inertia generated by capital's vested interests in the privileged capitalist countries and reformist labor's consensual complicity in their self-serving development, a triggering social upheaval is much more likely to take place in Latin America than in the United States or Western Europe, with far-reaching implications for the rest of the world.

In an interview in January 2003, *Folha de São Paulo*, the Brazilian national daily, asked me: "What is your opinion about the parallels traced between Luiz Inácio Lula da Silva and other Latin American leaders, such as Fidel Castro and Hugo Chávez?" This was my answer:

> The parallels are far-reaching, despite the obvious differences between the circumstances under which these radical leaders came to occupy their present position as heads of their respective governments. The parallels are dominant because they forcefully underline that the whole of Latin America is in need of a most profound, truly radical, change. . . . President Lula's landslide victory followed—by no means unconnectedly—the clamorous collapse of all attempted forms of accommodation in Argentina; a country considered for a very long time the unsurpassable model for Latin America. And when we speak about the three radical leaders: Lula, Fidel Castro, and Chávez, we should not forget President Allende, who also attempted to introduce radical change in his country, and had to perish for it. No doubt, those who refuse to contemplate the very idea of meaningful change will continue to try to wipe out the time of Latin American radical leaders appearing on the historical stage. But equally beyond doubt, such leaders are bound to arise, again and again, for as long as the profound social and historical reasons for their arrival are not positively attended to.

We can now add to the list of radical Latin American leaders the name of Evo Morales, who was elected President of Bolivia in a landslide victory in December 2005. His campaign was followed with great expectations by the popular masses of his country, especially because he was promising to carry out a far-reaching *Bolívarian Revolution*. The overwhelming support he received on account of his promised program is itself a clear indication of the strong desire in Bolivia for a radical change. In light of past disappointments, it remains to be seen if Morales can meet the expectations of his people, under undoubtedly very difficult circumstances. Whatever might be the verdict on that score, we can be absolutely certain that more and more radical political leaders will come forward throughout Latin America, including countries in which radical forces have suffered some major disappointments in the recent past as a result of their governments' craven accommodation to U.S. political and financial dictates. They are bound to come forward, in response to the deepening crisis of their societies as well as of the global capital system in general, with unavoidable commitment to instituting a viable alternative even against the most hostile obstructionism from abroad and the grave structural problems inherited from the past in their own countries. Only the articulation and intensification of a radical alternative—anchored in the broad masses of the people, with an uncompromising strategy pressing for a truly comprehensive transformation of society—can promise a way out of the all too obviously paralyzing maze of contradictions.

Naturally, it would be an illusion to expect a linear ascending development in this regard. We must soberly face the fact that the adversaries of socialism have enormous resources at their disposal for protecting capital's deeply entrenched power. This is the *negative* dimension of the great historical challenge we must face. At the same time, the *positive* requirement of a lasting success is even weightier. The elaboration of viable socialist strategies, as well as the successful articulation and consolidation of the corresponding organizational forms both internally and on the international plane, remain a fundamental challenge for the future. For these reasons, real setbacks and even major relapses cannot be excluded, no matter how great the need for positive solutions and how promising the initial achievements.

In Brazil, the radical wing of the working-class movement, both in the trade unions and in the political parties, played a crucial role in putting an end to its U.S.-sponsored military dictatorship well over two decades ago. In that way, it also inspired radical movements elsewhere in Latin America. Moreover, subsequently the Brazilian Workers' Party (PT) scored a major electoral success with Luiz Inácio Lula da Silva's rise to the Presidency. And yet, despite some undeniable tangible achievements in limited areas, capital's long-established order in Brazil succeeded in remaining firmly in control of the overall societal reproduction process, marginalizing its opponents also in politics, to the great disappointment of the popular forces in all parts of the country. Understandably, therefore, socialist militants in Brazil are compelled to argue today that there is still a long way to go before the inherited constraints of the organized historical left—which tended to be confined in *every* capitalist country to a political space and role thoroughly compatible with the mode of operation of the old order—could be considered to have been significantly altered, let alone to have been overcome on a lasting basis.

But even so, notwithstanding all identifiable and potential setbacks, it would be quite wrong to paint a pessimistic picture as regards the prospects of overall developments, concerning the continued viability (or not) of the capital system in its entirety. Despite capital's bewildering successes in the last two decades in different parts of the world, especially in the former societies of "actually existing socialism," it is very important to stress that the forces working for the institution of a radically different social order have found encouraging manifestations in several parts of the geopolitical backyard of the United States—not only in Venezuela but also in Colombia, where the militants continue to defy the most uneven odds.

Moreover, it is also of great significance that the radical social movements in different parts of the world, no matter how relatively weak they might be for the time being, are determined to shake off the historically generated but by now most anachronistic organizational limitations of the traditional political Left. They cannot accept any longer the easy explanation that the failure of some cherished past strategies, together with the corresponding implosion experienced by the socialist movement, was accidental or simply a matter of personal betrayals. Realizing that a critical—and self-critical—reexamination of some important past strategic and organizational assumptions is called for under the present historical circumstances, they are engaged in a painful but necessary process of reorienting their forces. They are trying to do this in order to be able to implement not only the necessary negation of the existent order but also the positive dimension of a sustainable *hegemonic alternative*. It is important to stress this circumstance so as to counter the ubiquitous propaganda of the established order, which continues to claim its permanent triumph over its erstwhile socialist adversaries.

When Prime Minister Margaret Thatcher, the devoted ideological and political adherent of neoliberalism in Britain, succeeded in defeating the British miners' year-long strike by ruthlessly deploying the full economic and police resources of the capitalist state, she boasted that she had *"seen off socialism for good."* This statement was a preposterous presumption, even if it seemed to be confirmed by the British Labour Party's eager capitulatory transformation into New Labour—the "friend of business" in the words of its leaders and preferably of Big Business at that. In reality, the relatively easy spread of neoliberalism from the 1970s onwards was not simply a British phenomenon but an overwhelming international development, extending in one way or another over the whole of our planet.

What is even more important to stress in this respect is that the ruthless enforcement of the main tenets of neoliberalism virtually everywhere on the planet—astonishingly, on the face of it, even in the societies of "actually existing socialism"—was not at all the manifestation of capital's irresistible revitalization and permanently secured health in the direction of the future. On the contrary, it was made necessary by the onset of the system's *structural crisis,* due to the dangerously *narrowing margins* of sustainable *capital-expansion.* To this qualitatively new structural crisis capital could only respond by assuming an ever more aggressive posture.

Accordingly, in the course of its development in the last three decades, capital has had to claw back the "concessions" of the welfare state earlier granted to labor (which it did not have to pay anything at all for at the time since the alleged concessions were part and parcel of the dynamics of the postwar period's undisturbed and highly profitable capital-expansion). The redefinition of the established order's strategic orientation in the spirit of callous neoliberalism was both the practical implementation of the ever more exploitative and repressive policies dictated by capital's harshly authoritarian turn and its cynical ideological justification.

Indeed, what makes these facts much worse for capital's devotees is that it is not possible to claim that through its openly authoritarian stance neoliberalism actually succeeded in solving the system's structural crisis by opening the doors to a new phase of healthy expansion, as repeatedly promised but never realized. The fact that in recent years the dominant powers of global capital have had to go as far as to engage in aggressive and catastrophically wasteful adventures, including the practice of unleashing genocidal wars, from which there seems to be "*no exit strategy*,"[23] demonstrates the utter failure of the attempted remedies and the significant worsening of the crisis itself.

Another dimension of the same problem directly concerns the prospects of the development of labor as the structural antagonist of capital. In contrast to all talk about the claimed integration of the working class, in actuality, we find the total misrepresentation of the—undoubtedly accomplished—capitulation of labor's traditional *political leadership* as the necessary and forever unalterable integration of the working *class itself*, i.e., as the irreversible integration of the one and only social force capable of offering a hegemonic alternative to the rule of capital. A rule which is no longer sustainable because of its increasingly destructive inner determinations.

Admittedly, the British Labour Party's capitulatory transformation into New Labour was by no means an isolated phenomenon. Some parties once upon a time well to the left of British Labour—for instance the Italian and the French Communist Parties—suffered in the same period an equally negative fate. The apologists of the established order celebrate all such metamorphoses in the same way as they greeted the successful imposition of neoliberalism everywhere. That is, as welcome evidence of the capitalist system's enduring revitalization and, consequently, as the unchallengeable triumph of the arbitrarily proclaimed wisdom according to which *there is no alternative.*

However, nothing could be a more myopic misreading of these events and developments which stand and fall together. The historical evidence itself points in the opposite direction not despite but, paradoxically, precisely because of the fact that the traditional mainstream forces of the Left in many countries subordinated themselves unreservedly to the dictates of capital in structural crisis. For the truth, uncomfortable though it may be to the defenders of the existing order, is that even the most slavish accommodation of the traditional labor leadership—devoid of a viable strategy of its own—is quite unable to remedy the situation. In this sense, the most disturbing truth is that nothing seems to work, even in the short term, under the present historical circumstances without the intensification of capital's socioeconomic aggressiveness and its direct extension into *growing state violence.*

What actually happened through the imposition of neoliberalism, with the most active contribution of reformist labor in several countries, was the irrevocable removal of the "grand illusion" according to which *class accommodation* and *gradual reform* were the only answers to society's grave *structural* problems. Projecting the necessary solution in this way—that is, by postulating the elimination of the capital *system's* grave *structural defects* through temporarily feasible and limited *gradual tinkering*—was, of course, a *contradiction in terms*. Naturally, this circumstance sealed the fate of "evolutionary socialism," although it took a long time before the promises of that mystifying approach had to be openly abandoned even by its leading proponents. The humiliating failure of the most accommodative strategies of reformist labor seen in all of history make it painfully obvious today that class accommodation and gradual reform were not answers to the established *social structure's* increasingly serious *systemic* problems.

The root cause of aggressive neoliberalism is the dangerously narrowing margin of undisturbed capital-expansion and conflict-attenuating growth, and thereby, the system's ever more constrained ability for managing, without destructive adventurism, its major structural problems, notwithstanding the active complicity of formerly reformist labor on the side of neoliberal capital. All of this underlines the severity of the crisis of our time and the total absurdity of all talk about "seeing off socialism for good." For undisturbed *capital-expansion*—in conjunction with *conflict-attenuating growth*—and the unchallenged *submissive accommodation* of reformist labor to capital's rule are two sides of the same coin.

Once the road to undisturbed and sustainable capital-expansion is narrowed and ultimately blocked by the deepening structural crisis of the system, the principal motivating force for labor's willing self-accommodation is bound to be weakened as the facts begin to sink in. This is so, even if at the beginning of such a downward spiral the leadership of reformist labor tries to do everything it can in order to mitigate the negative and ultimately destabilizing consequences of capital's failure to deliver the goods. It adopts an unreservedly and humiliatingly obsequious position toward capital, in the vain hope of successfully contributing to the system's revitalization and healthy functioning. Naturally, under such circumstances the tired old mantra of "left-

Keynesianism" is recited again and again. But there can be nothing to confer reality upon it.

Thus, both the permanence of neoliberalism (often associated with the grotesque pseudo-theory which preaches the happy "ending of history") and the proclaimed absolute necessity of labor's eternal self-accommodation are nothing more than disorienting *optical illusions,* projected much to the convenience of the established order. They are temporarily reinforced from two directions. On one side, by neoliberalism's well understandable positive embrace of its newfound ideal interlocutor, capitulatory labor. And on the other side, by self-accommodating labor's need for a somewhat mythically aggrandized (powerful but reasonable and benevolent) adversary, promoted to the status of a veritable "partner" who is now respectfully described as the "producer of wealth," despite the increasing parasitism of its now dominant dimension: speculative finance capital. This is done by reformist labor in order to justify, before its electoral followers, its open complicity with the perpetuation of the harshly exploitative order as it stands. It is by now not in the slightest embarrassed about having abandoned its erstwhile reformist aspirations for "gradual change" toward an equitable alternative order on the even more vacuously proclaimed ground that "there is no alternative."

In reality, however, the vital need for a *hegemonic alternative* to capital's rule has appeared on the historical agenda for some time. All known modalities of reformist accommodation—across one hundred and thirty years of history (from the time of the "Gotha Program")—have failed to make the slightest lasting impact on the grave contradictions and inhumanities of the capitalist system. This state of affairs could be maintained, notwithstanding the system's antagonisms and inhumanities, for as long as capital could impose itself—when possible with the help of productive achievements, when not by naked force—as the unchallenged controller of societal reproduction. But it is precisely this which is becoming extremely problematic in our own time. Extremely problematical indeed—partly because even capital's most authoritarian posture, coupled with reformist labor's totally submissive accommodation, has failed to produce the promised healthy economic expansion. And even more importantly, because the ongoing aggressive and adventurist developments unmistakably put into relief capital's perilous drive towards humanity's destruction—all in the irrational interest of the established reproductive order's survival at any cost, to which capital truly *cannot conceive*, let alone *concede*, any alternative.

Following the line of least resistance is, by definition, always much easier than fighting for the institution of a really feasible hegemonic alternative. For the latter requires not only active commitment to the cause chosen by the participants but also their acceptance of likely sacrifices. This is the greatest asset of our adversaries and underlines the vital importance of the elaboration and implementation of viable political and social strategies in order to counter the significant positional advantage of institutionalized inertia. The necessary removal of the disorienting optical illusions mentioned above—namely, the absolute permanence of neoliberalism and of labor's beneficial self-accommodation to it—is not possible without both full awareness of how high the stakes for securing humanity's survival really are in our time and practical engagement in the required fundamental transformation of the existing social order in its entirety, in the spirit of *radical determination*.

Tinkering here and there, in our time, leads absolutely nowhere. It can only reinforce the positional advantage of those who are now in control of the historically anachronistic capital system. In other words, countering with success the mystifications of neoliberal invincibility, actively sustained by accommodative labor, is not simply a question of ideological enlightenment. The battle cannot be won on the terrain of political persuasion alone, since consistently critical convictions often coexist with practical powerlessness. Lasting success is feasible only through the organizationally sustainable mobilization of the great masses of the people for the realization of an *all-embracing hegemonic alternative* to the established mode of social metabolic reproduction.

The spirit of radical determination today is inseparable from a firm commitment—as required by the need to confront the dangerous historical developments—to the institution of the envisaged hegemonic alternative to capital's increasingly adventurist and destructive rule. This is why President Chávez repeatedly stressed both the inescapability of the dilemma of *socialism or barbarism* in our time and the corresponding necessity to engage in the only feasible form of successful action: a sustained *strategic offensive,* given the magnitude and the literally vital urgency of the

historical task. In his intervention at the January 2003 World Social
Forum in Porto Allegre, Chávez rightly warned against the harmful temptation of allowing the worldwide meetings of the major emerging social
movements to turn into annually ritualized *folkloric events*. And he repeated the same warning at the January 2006 World Social Forum in Caracas,
insisting that such transformation of the potentially radical social movements into a *"touristic/folkloric encounter would be terrible, because we
would be simply wasting time, and we have no time to waste.* I believe that
it is not given to us to speak in terms of future centuries . . . we have no
time to waste; the challenge is to save the conditions of life on this planet,
to save the human species, to change the course of history, to change the
world."[24]

In order to meet the radically new historical challenge of our time,
which puts into question the very survival of humanity, the original
Bolívarian project is necessarily modified in two of its fundamental
dimensions. In the first respect, the required qualitative change directly affects the all-important question of *equality*. In the second respect, it
must address the unresolved dilemma of even the greatest and most radical political thinkers of the Enlightenment, including Rousseau (who
was in many ways the model for Bolívar himself). Namely: how to overcome on a lasting basis—or at least how to bring to a common denominator, sustainable for an unavoidable period of transition—the conflicting and potentially disintegration producing interests at work in
society.

These two fundamental dimensions of a historically workable solution to humanity's great dilemmas—which appeared in their first utopian
formulations thousands of years before the Age of Enlightenment but
have remained frustrated and sidelined ever since—are closely intertwined. The potentially explosive contradictions and mutually exclusive
interests perpetuated by the long-established antagonistic social structure
can not be overcome without finding a viable solution—in a *substantive
way*—to the historically, up to the present, intractable problem of equality. Every form of (in principle reversible) legal enactment can only scratch
the surface of this problem. And vice versa: it is inconceivable to find a
substantive, and thereby *legally nonreversible,* solution to the seminal
issue of equality, upon which all of the other commendable social values

rest—in Bolívar's memorable words, "from all freedoms to all rights," including justice—without permanently relegating to the historical past the conflicts and antagonisms necessarily generated and reproduced in one form or another by the structurally and hierarchically entrenched and safeguarded *substantive* (and not just legally codified) social relations.

In the deepest sense of the issues at stake, the two fundamental dimensions of humanity's great dilemmas are one and the same, distinguishable partly because this is how they were treated in past political discourse. And more importantly, they must be distinguished for the purpose of elaborating a practically feasible as well as lasting—and now historically both possible and necessary—solution to society's explosive contradictions. However in light of past disappointments, we must be aware of the fact that in their innermost substance they are inseparable. It was due to the past disregard for their substantive inseparability that even the noblest intentions for overcoming the violations of equality through legislative reform (which may well be necessary as a vital first step under determinate historical circumstances),[25] and leaving at the same time the entrenched *substantive structural hierarchies* in their place in society, had to suffer major reversals sooner or later.

We have to recall in this respect that for Bolívar equality was *"the law of laws"* because "without equality all freedoms, all rights perish. For it we must make sacrifices." Defining the problem in this way was Bolívar's direct appeal to the spirit of *enlightenment and morality* in his fellow legislators. Consider his characterization of the two cardinal requirements of a politically viable form of legislation in his Address before the Congress of Angostura: "Morality and enlightenment are the poles of a Republic; morality and enlightenment are our primary necessities."[26] Although this was an undoubtedly valid formulation of some vital political guiding principles in their given social setting, Bolívar's way of defining the problem of equality as *legally enacted equality*, dependent on the enlightened insight and moral sympathy of his fellow legislators (many of them, in fact, quite unwilling to make the stipulated sacrifices), had inevitably imposed strict limitations even on Bolívar's radical approach. Indeed, the qualifications expressed by him on some occasion indicated, at least by implication, his awareness of the social limits of the actually accomplished level of equality.[27] After all, even the legal emancipation of the slaves could be subsequently nullified by a variety of legally devised pseudo-contractual alternatives, which cynically retained many features of former slavery, including the brutally enslaving arrangement called indentured labor; not to mention the *substantive triumph of wage slavery* everywhere, glorified in the annals of liberal political economy as "free labor." And another sobering note: under the circumstances prevailing in Bolívar's lifetime in Latin America, even the degree of social and political radicalism advocated by him proved to be far too much for many of his contemporaries.

As regards *substantive equality*,[28] its realization is undoubtedly the greatest and the most difficult of all historic tasks. Accordingly, real advancement in the direction of substantive equality becomes feasible only when the *objective material conditions* of its realization—including society's historically achieved *positive productive potentiality*—are appropriately matched at the level of ideas and values. The latter may well be called the *spiritual conditions* of overcoming the age-old social hierarchies which have been reinforced by the culture of *substantive inequality*, even in the writings of some very great intellectuals of the progressive bourgeoisie. Given these circumstances, success is feasible only if some vital conditions are historically satisfied. On the one hand, the "equitable distribution of misery," in the absence of favorable material requirements, cannot be socially sustained as a condition of normality for any length of time. On the other hand, the pretended achievement of "material abundance"—i. e., the pernicious myth of "the affluent society"—cannot solve anything if a genuine dedication to mutually beneficial solidarity (and associated values) is missing, for whatever reason, from individuals' conception of productive advancement, irrespective of how high the available level of technological and scientific know-how might be under the circumstances. In the absence of values which enable the development of rich individuality, in place of the all-around dominant antagonistic competitiveness, all fetishistically celebrated material abundance is invariably transformed into never to be eliminated *scarcity*. Thereby, the self-justifying vicious circle of wasteful "progress" toward the irrational conversion of ever greater *productive potentiality* into *destructive reality* can go on unhindered until a global catastrophe brings it to a halt.

BOLÍVAR AND CHÁVEZ   143

This is the point where we can see the line separating us from the past in which concern with equality could only be pursued, even by the most enlightened statesmen, as a legally defined political objective. This had to be the case when the issues at stake carried important social connotations, such as the formal liberation—but by no means the actual socioeconomic emancipation—of the slaves. The radical novelty of our condition of existence, in the present historical epoch, is that there can be no lasting success in the struggle for humanity's survival without the establishment of a *social order* based on *substantive equality* as its central orienting principle on the terrain of both *production* and *distribution*. This is so because capital's incorrigible *destructiveness* affects every single facet of our life: from the irresponsible wastefulness of profit-oriented productive pursuits to the suicidal degradation of nature as well as the irreversible exhaustion of its vital reproductive resources; and from the dehumanizing mass production of superfluous people, in the form of chronic unemployment, to the most extreme varieties of current military adventurism. Accompanying this military adventurism is the outrageous justification of nothing less than the use of nuclear weapons by the dominant imperialist country, the United States, done not only retrospectively, with regard to the unforgivable deed against the people of Hiroshima and Nagasaki, but in a most sinister way also in relation to the future. The traditional advocacy by capital's personifications "to think the unthinkable"—in their self-congratulatory spirit which claims the virtues of successfully accomplished "productive destruction"—finds its ultimate realization in a form in which *contemplating and threatening the destruction of humanity,* absurdly in the interest of the ruling socioeconomic system's survival at any cost, is *legitimated* as a necessary *strategic objective* by capital's most powerful state formation.

At the root of all of these destructive manifestations we find the insurmountable imperatives arising from the established order's self-perpetuating *structural hierarchies,* which necessarily exclude any comprehensive *rational alternative* to capital's mode of social metabolic control. Naturally, considerations of substantive equality cannot conceivably enter capital's framework of decision-making when the fundamentals are at stake. This makes the structural crisis of our system of social reproductive control uniquely acute at the present historical juncture, indicating at the same time the only feasible way of overcoming it. For the destructive determinations of the established order, erupting everywhere on a devastating scale and with a previously inconceivable gravity, now call for a fundamental *structural change* in the interest of humanity's survival.

Structurally enforced inequality is the all-important defining characteristic of the capital system, without which it could not function for a single day. The institution of the required *fundamental structural change* makes it necessary to produce a *substantively equitable alternative* as humanity's only viable future mode of social metabolic control. There could not conceivably be a higher stake for human beings than securing and safeguarding the survival and positive advancement of humankind. The possibility of instituting a humanly fulfilling order of *substantive social equality* is, under the present conditions, not an *abstract possibility* but a *vital necessity*.

For this reason, in sharp contrast to their adversaries, the forces dedicated to this great historic task can pursue the realization of their objective with rationality fully on their side, confident of the complete justification of the values advocated by them in their struggle against imperialism, monopoly, and oppression. Truly, we live in an age that might be called the clash of imperatives, although by no means "the clash of civilizations." The critical confrontation of our time asserts itself as the imperative for creating an equitable and sustainable social order. That is, an order which is historically sustainable precisely because of its innermost determination as equitable in all of its substantive dimensions—as against capital's insurmountable imperative of destructive self-preservation. In view of the nature of the issues involved and the urgency of their pursuit, there has never been an even remotely comparable prospect for turning into reality the age-old advocacy of substantive equality as the primary determination of human interchange.

In this sense also the reasons for the chronically unresolved question of how to overcome on a lasting basis the conflicting and potentially disintegration producing interests at work in society must be reexamined. The answer given in the past, even by the most enlightened statesmen, including Bolívar, was to politically *balance* the diverse social forces, so as "to maintain the *equilibrium* not only among the members of the government but also among the different fractions constituting our society."[29] In the end, such a strategy had to turn out to be fragile even in its own terms of reference, resulting in periodic convulsions and reversals in its political setting despite the fact that what was at stake concerned only the partial redefinition and redistribution of the *relative share* of the diverse social forces in the structurally given power relations. However, the hierarchical structural parameters of the given social order were themselves not questioned. On the contrary, they had to be taken for granted by the orienting principles of *"balancing"* and *"equilibrium."* By contrast, today the radical questioning of the structural parameters of the established social system is the order of the day. For, evidently, even the most skilful political balancing of the social forces under the rule of capital cannot undertake the task of instituting the required *fundamental structural change,* no matter how acute the need for it, as happens to be the case today. This is why only the consistent pursuit of the objective to establish a social order of substantive equality can meet the historical challenge in our time, under the conditions of the capital system's irreversible structural crisis.

As we have seen, toward the end of his life Bolívar was forced to concede that, tragically, the day of America, as he had envisaged it before, had not yet arrived. Today the situation is very different, due to a number of major determinations. In other words, Bolívar's "day of America" has arrived in the sense that the age-old conditions of Latin America's quasi-colonial domination by the United States cannot be perpetuated in the future. In this regard, the interest in the socioeconomic freedom and politically effective national sovereignty of the Latin American countries fully coincides with the necessary drive for overcoming national grievances everywhere. The long prevailing national domination of many countries by a few imperialist powers has become an irremediable historical anachronism.

This new historical condition cannot be undone by the fact that the former imperialist powers, and the most powerful of them all by far, the United States, are trying to turn back the wheel of history and *recolonize* the world. Their design is already visible in the devastating military adventures advanced under the pretext of the so-called war against terror. Indeed, the new panacea of the most aggressive powers is that embarking on what does in fact amount to a blatant re-colonizing venture—in Africa and Southeast Asia, as well as in Latin America—is declared by them to be the essential condition of success in their cynical "war against terror." They are bound to fail in this enterprise.

In the past, many efforts aimed at rectifying justifiable national griev- ances were derailed by the pursuit of chauvinistic strategies. Given the nature of the problems at stake, repressed *national* interests cannot pre- vail at the expense of the viable social objectives of some other nations, thereby violating the required *fully equitable international conditions* of inter-state relations. Thus, the far-sighted historical validity of the Bolívarian project, pressing for the strategic unity and equality of the Latin American countries not simply against the United States but also within the broader framework of an envisaged harmonious international association of all, could not be clearer. By realizing social and political unity based on their solidarity, the Latin American countries can play a pioneering role today, in the interest of the whole of humankind. None of them can succeed in isolation even negatively, against their powerful antagonist in North America, but together they can show a way forward to all of us in an exemplary fashion. For only the historically appropriate renewal and consistent pursuit of a strategy capable of bringing the national and the international dimensions of social interchange to their positive common denominator everywhere, in the spirit of radical deter- mination, can solve the grave structural crisis of our social order.

CHAPTER SIX

The Importance of Planning and Substantive Equality[1]

6.1 The "Invisible Hand" and the "Cunning of Reason"

Planning occupies a most important place among the categories of socialist theory. This is in sharp contrast to the capital system in which—due to the *centrifugal* inner determination of its productive and distributive microcosms—there is no real scope for planning in the full sense of the term. That sense must be defined both as *consciously pursued comprehensive planning of production and distribution* and, at the same time, as going well beyond the limitations of *technical and technological* coordination, no matter how broadly based.

Naturally, the great thinkers who conceptualized the world from capital's vantage point realized that something *essential* was missing from their depiction of the established reproductive order, without which it could not be sustained at all on a lasting basis, let alone qualify for being idealized as the one and only natural mode of humanity's social metabolic reproduction, as they declared it to be. Thus, as a striking but utterly mysterious afterthought, they introduced the idea of the "Invisible Hand" (Adam Smith), the "Commercial Spirit" (Kant), and the "Cunning of Reason" (Hegel).

Such a mysterious *supra-individual* entity, irrespective of its name, was supposed to achieve what in a non-antagonistically structured human society should be accomplished by freely determined *comprehensive planning*. And the projected supra-individual agency was supposed to fulfill the task of overall coordination and direction incomparably better, by definition, than particular individuals could even dream about.

In the conceptions formulated from capital's vantage point, two—*irreconcilable*—conditions had to be satisfied. First, there is the *retention* of political economy's mythology of "civil society" (abstracted from the capitalist state), with its insoluble *individual* antagonism, quarrelsomeness, and conflicts. (All of this is appropriate to Kant's "crooked timber" —"out of the crooked timber of humanity no straight thing was ever made"—from which particular individuals were supposed to have been made by Providence, nature-determined or Divine.) Hence, particular individuals could not possibly be entrusted with the vital task of securing the orderly cohesion of reproductive activity in society, without which the new economic order would fall to pieces.

And the second condition that had to be satisfied was the production of overall societal cohesion. This process was contradictorily posited in the form of reasserting what the thinkers in question considered to be the objective ontological determinations of insuperably conflictual civil society. An imaginary solution to the insuperable conflicts of civil society was offered by transubstantiating the *negative* interchange of particularistic self-seeking competition as such into the *positive* benefits that were supposed to arise from the conflicts themselves for the *whole*. Whereby, in Hegel's words, thanks to a miraculous "dialectical" advance, *"subjective self-seeking* turns into a contribution to the satisfaction of the needs of *everyone else."* So it is apologetically decreed by the great German philosopher.[2] This kind of beneficial transmutation of the negative into the positive, to be realized in a postulated but never explained or demonstrated way, was celebrated by thinkers who viewed the world from capital's standpoint as the *ideal* harmonization of the societal reproduction process in its entirety. Only a mysterious supra-individual agency—be that Adam Smith's "Invisible Hand," Kant's "Commercial Spirit," or Hegel's "Cunning of Reason"—could accomplish such *ideal reconciliation* of the *irreconcilable*.

Thus, the projection of the supra-individual agency—in place of the required social organ of *comprehensive planning,* instituted by freely associated *social* (and not isolated self-seeking) individuals—could create from the standpoint of political economy the *appearance* of solving the real problem. But even for creating that appearance only, it was necessary to misrepresent, first, the *fundamental social antagonism* of capitalist *class* society as the strictly *individual* conflict prevailing in eternalized civil society. And second, it was necessary to characterize the stipulated *object* of conflict itself, over which people had to confront each other, as simply a matter of *individual enjoyment,* pertaining to the sphere of *consumption,* and thus *quantitatively* extendable—in Hegel's words to "everyone else." In this way, the *class* determined and *structurally enforced hierarchical division of labor*—which constitutes the real ground of the capital system's irreconcilable and ultimately explosive fundamental antagonism—could be left at its place in society as before. And, paradoxically, this *dual* misrepresentation of the problem was to a remarkable extent justified, in the sense of being theoretically consistent.

It was theoretically consistent precisely as a dual distortion. On the one hand, from capital's vantage point, it was necessary to misrepresent the real nature of insuperable *class* antagonism—deeply inherent in, and thus for its solution requiring the radical change of, the historically given *structural* framework of society—as purely *individual* conflicts in civil society, whose reconciliation would not call for any *structural change* in the really existing society. On the other hand, it was also necessary to tendentiously depict the real object of conflict—the historical confrontation over two, incompatible, hegemonic alternative modes of *production,* as a straightforward matter of individual *consumption,* whose magnitude could be enlarged through the readily quantifiable exchange-value of capital's self-expansionary production process. These two major aspects of the capital system's structural determinations were always closely interconnected. Thus, opting for one, from capital's vantage point, in tune with the absolutely necessary exclusion of any idea of structural change in the established mode of production, carried with it the requirement of embracing also the other: i.e., the confinement of all feasible remedial adjustments to the sphere of individual consumption. In this sense, there could be really no alternative way of conceptualizing the problems at stake from the standpoint of capital's political economy. For it would be inconceivable to institute in the actually existing world the required historic alternative—that is, the comprehensive planning of the reproduction process—without *qualitatively* overcoming on a sustainable basis the *structurally* enforced hierarchical *division of labor* through a consciously manageable *organization of labor* in a communal organic system.

But even the mysterious supra-individual entity could not overcome the *post festum* character of planning: the only kind of planning feasible within the incurably fetishistic framework of capital's social metabolic control. The *corrective functions* envisaged in that system, through the operation of the idealized market, fail to qualify as genuine planning in two important ways. First, because they can only be *retroactive,* in response to perceived and—however reluctantly—after the event acknowledged miscalculations and failures. And second, given the very nature of their retroactive modality, they can only be *partial,* without any insight into the potentially far-reaching connections and ramifications of the acknowledged particular instances. Accordingly, *overall foresight*—a vital defining characteristic of consciously pursued comprehensive planning in the proper sense of the term—has no role. The necessary prerequisite for the realization of such a vital characteristic is the actual supersession of *adversarial relations.* This can be achieved by both overcoming, under the historically given circumstances, the established and necessarily disruptive *vested interests* and by *preventing,* through the appropriate *structural change* in society, their reconstitution in the future.

The political economist's conception of the world *had* to idealize the adversarial relations of egotistic vested interests, in their *individualistic* manifestations in civil society, in order to be able to (more or less consciously) divert attention from, and thus legitimate and eternalize by proxy capital's *structurally entrenched* vested interests of societal reproductive control. As such, the political economist had no conceivable way of satisfying the conditions required for the realization of overall foresight in planning, even as a mysterious remedial afterthought. This explains also why—even under the conditions of globally pursued monopolistic developments and irrespective of how large the transnational corporations brought into being through the irresistibly advancing concentration and centralization of capital might grow—the purported rationalizing solution of this fundamental defect of the capital system can only produce *partial* and largely technical and technological *post festum* "planning," without the ability to remedy the underlying structural antagonisms.

Naturally, a genuine socialist planning process is unthinkable without overcoming the fetishism of the commodity, with its perverse *quantification* of all human relations and activities. To be really meaningful, the criteria of socialist planning must be defined in *qualitative* terms. This means not simply improving the productive viability of general economic processes but also directly enriching, in human terms, the life of the particular social individuals. This is the sense in which Marx was talking about the "rich human being" and "rich human need," in contrast to the fetishistic conception of wealth and poverty advanced by political economy. Marx insisted that: "The *rich* human being is . . . the human being *in need of a totality of human life-activities*—the man in whom his own realization exists as an inner necessity, as *need.*"[3]

This is why the communal system would have to define itself in terms of the exchange of *activities*, in direct opposition to the exchange of commodities under the rule of capital. For the fetishism of commodities prevails in capital's social metabolic order in such a way that commodities *superimpose* themselves on *need,* measuring and legitimating (or callously denying the legitimacy of) human need. This is what we are accustomed to as the normative horizon of our everyday life. The obvious alternative is to have the products themselves subjected to some meaningful criteria of evaluation on the basis of which they would be produced in response to real need and above all in accordance, with the individuals' basic need for *humanly fulfilling life-activity.* However, such considerations simply cannot enter the framework of capitalist cost accounting because the organization and exercise of humanly fulfilling life-activity is an inherently *qualitative* concern (the judges of which can only be the social individuals themselves). As a result, we are not expected even to think about productive activities as belonging to the category of need. Naturally, even less are we expected to envisage the possibility of adopting the necessary practical measures through which we could reshape productive social intercourse on a *qualitative* basis, in harmony with the objectives which we, as freely associated producers, would set ourselves in order to gratify and further develop our genuine needs and realize our aspirations.

If we define planning in this *qualitative* way, in its vital correlation to human need, it acquires a direct relevance in the life of every individual. Here, we have a relationship of dialectical reciprocity between the social and the individual dimension of planning. Neither of the two can work without the other. The reciprocity in question means that in close consonance with the role which planning has to fulfill in the overall societal reproduction process, it simultaneously also challenges individuals to create a *meaningful* life of their own, as the real *subjects of their life-activity*. It challenges them to make sense of their own life, as real *authors* of their own acts, in conjunction with the developing potentialities of their society of which they are themselves an integral and actively contributing part. And this reciprocity must prevail also in another sense. Only if the social individuals become real subjects of their life-activity and freely assume responsibility for their own acts in the overall social enterprise, can the general planning process lose its remoteness from the—no longer recalcitrant—particular individuals, who can fully identify themselves with the overall objectives and values of their society. In this way, nothing could be further removed from the bureaucratic conception of planning, imposed on individuals from above. On the contrary, through the dialectical reciprocity of qualitatively defined planning, individual and social consciousness can really come together in the interest of positive human advancement. Indeed, this is how it becomes possible to constitute an alternative social metabolic order on a historically sustainable time scale. And that is what confers its true meaning on planning as a vital principle of the socialist enterprise.

6.2 The Long Historical Gestation of the Categories of Socialist Theory

Many of the categories of socialist theory, envisaging a positive solution to humanity's apparently intractable problems, have had a very long historical period of gestation. Some were advocated thousands of years ago, including the idea of communal living, but were prevented from getting anywhere near their possible realization; partly because of insufficient productive development and partly because of the stubbornly persisting antagonisms of interchange across the overall trajectory of class societies. The exploitation and domination of the overwhelming majority of the people by a small minority was not invented by capital. It only perfected a particular variety of structurally enforced economic, political, and cultural domination, asserting itself in its general tendency on a global scale, in contrast to the more particularistic and far less efficient historical predecessors of the capitalist system.

This makes the challenge of viable socialist transformation that much more difficult. Partial improvements—which leave the long established structural framework of inequality in its place, as regularly happened in the move from one form of class society to another in the past—are woefully inadequate. Nor is it feasible today to conveniently separate the "historical layers" of exploitative domination from one another, attending, in the vain hope of all-embracing success, only to the relatively recent ones through chosen legal devices. We had to learn a very bitter lesson in that regard in the course of the twentieth century. For it proved to be totally insufficient to "expropriate the expropriators"—the private capitalists— by means of state-legislative measures in Soviet-type post-capitalist societies, instituted for the announced objective of emancipating labor.

There can hardly be any doubt that the attainment of the highest level of productivity under the conditions of socialist development is necessary in order to satisfy human need, which has been denied on a massive scale in the course of history. Understandably, therefore, no matter how well intentioned, any call for an equitable distribution of misery could only prove self-defeating. As forcefully underlined by Marx and Engels in *The German Ideology*, "this development of productive forces . . . is an absolutely necessary practical premise, because without it privation, want is merely made general, and with want the struggle for necessities would begin again, and all the old filthy business would necessarily be restored."[4] Today, in contrast to the precarious conditions of the more remote past, sometimes naïvely idealized in utopian theories, the productive requirements of humanity's emancipation can be conquered. But they must be *conquered* by radically overcoming capital's wastefully and destructively articulated productive system before feasible potentialities can be turned into realities, fit for the purpose of emancipatory transformation.

At the dawn of the modern age, one of the historic aspirations pointing in the direction of a future socialist transformation was concerned with the question of productive activity itself. A most original and radical thinker of the sixteenth century, Paracelsus—one of Goethe's historical models of the "Faustian spirit"—wrote that: "The proper way resides in work and action, in doing and producing; the perverse man does nothing."[5] According to him, labor (*arbeit*) had to be adopted as the ordering principle of society in general, to the extent of even confiscating the wealth of the idle rich, in order to compel them to lead a productive life.[6] However, the realization of such orienting principles always depends on the actual historical conditions and on the way in which the projected changes are sustainable in the overall framework of society. It was, therefore, by no means surprising that Marx sharply criticized the approach adopted by "crude and thoughtless communism"[7] to this problem. He pointed out that in such a crude approach: "The category of *labour* is not done away with, but *extended to all men*. The relationship of *private property* persists as the relationship of the *community* to the *world of things*."[8] Thus, the totally untenable postulate of "crude communism" was the retention of the alienating private property system while imagining to overcome it by extending the condition of labor to all men. In this way, self-contradictorily, "the community is only a community of *labour,* and an equality of *wages* paid out by the communal capital—the *community* as the universal capitalist. Both sides of the relationship are raised to an *imagined* universality—*labour* as a state in which every person is put, and *capital* as the acknowledged universality and power of the community."[9]

The extension of *productive activity* to all members of society is, of course, a vital principle of the socialist organization of society. But it could not be imagined as the imposition of *labor*—inherited from capital's mode of societal reproduction—with its *fetishistic and quantifying wage determinations from above*, even if positing an "equality of wages." What was entirely missing from the conception of crude and thoughtless communism was an understanding of the *differentia specifica* of the actually given *historical* conditions under which transformative changes had to be made and the need for the supersession of the antagonistic relations between capital and labor through the substantive *abolition* of private property, and not for its imaginary enhancement. These objective requirements were missing from the postulates of crude communism, and without them it was unthinkable to take the necessary steps towards the emancipation of labor in the only feasible *qualitative* way. The only sense in which a—qualitatively different—conception of labor, as *self-determined productive activity*, can be extended to all members of society is through realization of the positive vision of freely associated social individuals, "*in need of a totality of human life-activities*,"[10] fulfilling their autonomously determined tasks in community with each other on the basis of their *inner* necessity, their real *need*.

Equality is another category of fundamental socialist relevance with a very long period of historical gestation. Understandably, it is closely connected with the question of genuinely self-fulfilling productive activity in the life of individuals. To be sure, it was originally conceived as *substantive* equality. For it was advocated as a type of human relationship suitable to significantly diminish discriminatory constraints and contradictions, thereby enriching the life of individuals not only in material terms but also as a result of introducing a greater degree of fairness and justice in their interchanges with one another. Of course, there was also an obvious *class* aspect to these concerns, arguing in favor of the elimination of some pre-established and ossified measures and rules of subjection and subordination. It postulated the improvement of the general conditions of well being in society, thanks to a more enlightened and less conflict-torn management of its problems. This is in contrast to later *reversals*, which, in diametrical opposition, asserted that any attempt at spreading equality would unavoidably result in a *leveling down* and thus bring with it the creation of *insuperable conflicts*.

The aprioristically disqualifying accusations, which asserted the necessary connection between introducing a greater degree of substantive equality and the *equitable distribution of misery*, were a typical manifestation of this line of approach, reflecting the actually existing relation of forces overwhelmingly on the side of the iniquitous established order. The brutal liquidation of François Babeuf's secret "Society of Equals" was also a clear indication of how the fate of those pressing for substantive equality was sealed with the entrenchment of the new forms of inequality in the aftermath of the French Revolution. Capital's stabilized socioeconomic order, firmly securing the *structural subordination* of the subjected class of labor, could not offer scope for anything but the most restricted measures of strictly *formal* equality, confined to the legitimation of the *contractual* subjugation of the workers to the dominant material interests. This is how one of the great promises of the Enlightenment ended as a distant memory of a noble illusion.

However, this is by no means the end of the story. For with the appearance of organized labor on the historical stage, with its claim to be the carrier of a viable and hegemonic alternative socioeconomic, political, and cultural order, the issue of substantive equality has been reopened in a radically different way. It has been reopened in the form of asserting not the *equality of classes* but the necessity to put an end altogether to *class inequality as such* through the establishment of a *classless society*. Accordingly, the issue is defined in this revived form as the most emphatic advocacy of *substantive equality*. And this is not a *desideratum*. For the fact is that the envisaged socialist social order is totally unworkable in any other way. In other words, the alternative in this respect is that either the idea of instituting a qualitatively different—classless—social metabolic order must be abandoned as an untenable illusion, just like the great illusions of the Enlightenment, or it must be practically articulated and firmly consolidated in all of its major aspects as a historically sustainable society based on *substantive equality*.

6.3 The Key Role of Substantive Equality

There are compelling reasons for presenting the issue in the form of this stark alternative. Those who maintain a concern with the realization of substantive equality are called hopeless "idealists" and "utopian dreamers" tied to the remnants of an Enlightenment illusion. Such accusations are not just conveniently fashionable, even though they certainly are. There is a much more serious aspect to this kind of critique. In its fallacious apologetics for the established order, it purports to be in no need of proving and substantiating its categorically dismissive position, and it assumes that a vacuous disqualifying reference to an allegedly buried past (the Enlightenment and its unforgivable illusions) makes any proof utterly superfluous. This is a favorite methodological device employed in the service of justifying the unjustifiable.

In this way, a vital terrain of important theoretical contestation is arbitrarily ruled out of bounds. This on account of it simply being connected with an intellectual tradition which in its time tried to genuinely respond to major problems and grievances, even if it was unable to do so without postulating its own illusions for solving them. The fact that the disqualified past—dismissed in the more or less visibly camouflaged interest of disqualifying the present—belongs to the long *historical gestation* of a *socially irrepressible* concern cannot even be mentioned. Nor can it be mentioned that a legitimate critique of the Enlightenment should investigate *why* its solutions had to be in many ways illusory, due to the *underlying class determinations*. What must be hidden from sight is the circumstance that the issue of equality itself concerns a strategically crucial orienting principle of the *necessary qualitative transformation* of the untenable established order. This is the case even if the imperative of that order's radical supersession, oriented by the principle of not formal but *substantive equality*, can only be spelled out at the present stage of historical development in the form of our stark alternative. By aprioristically disqualifying all concern with equality, they can easily do the same with all of the other seminal orienting principles of a sustainable socialist transformation of society closely linked to the requirements of substantive equality.

Redefining the fundamental conditions of an historically viable alternative mode of social metabolic reproduction in accordance with the principle of substantive equality is an essential part of socialist strategy. For substantive equality is not just *one* of the many orienting principles of the socialist enterprise. It occupies a *key* position within the general framework of labor's hegemonic alternative to the established societal reproductive order. Nearly all of the other vital orienting principles of socialist strategy can only acquire their *full meaning* in close conjunction with the requirement of substantive equality. Not in an *absolute* sense, of course, in that neither a *structural* primacy nor a *historical* antecedence could be asserted in favor of substantive equality, as against the other important defining characteristics of socialist strategy, since we are concerned here with a set of dialectical interrelations and reciprocal determinations.

Nevertheless, as we shall see, substantive equality occupies the position of *primus inter pares* (i.e., the position of the "first among equals") in this complex relationship of dialectical reciprocity, which is not only

compatible with but also *required* by the historically unfolding, and reciprocally enriching, dialectical correlation in question. The other categorial
orienting principles are not *less important* or *more negligible* but *more specific* and context-bound than substantive equality. To put it in more
explicit terms, they all have a fairly direct connection with substantive
equality, but not necessarily with each other, except through complicated
indirect mediations among themselves. This is why substantive equality
can and must occupy the position of *primus inter pares* in an overall complex of strategic development from which *none* of the others can be omit-
ted, nor indeed could they be even temporarily neglected for the sake of
convenience.

Here are the principal classes in which the particular categories and
orienting principles of the socialist strategic enterprise can be thematical-
ly related to each other, concerning:

1.   the question of the established order's structurally prevailing *antag-
      onisms* and the hegemonic alternative way of organizing social meta-
      bolic reproduction;

2.   the operating principles required for the realization of an historical-
      ly sustainable form of *productive* activity in an hegemonic alternative
      order and the type of *distribution* in harmony with that kind of soci-
      etal reproduction;

3.   the relationship between the categorial principles of *negation—vis-
      à-vis* capital's ruling social metabolic order—and the *inherently pos-
      itive* articulation of the historic alternative; and

4.   the categorial connection between the inherited, dominant *values* of
      society, together with the positive definition of the advocated alter-
      natives, as well as the reassessment of the relationship between *indi-
      vidual and social consciousness,* including the thorny issue of "false
      consciousness."

In all four classes the connection of the particular categories and orienting principles with substantive equality is very clear.

(1) One of the most compelling reasons why labor's hegemonic alternative order is sustainable only on the basis of the institution and ongoing consolidation of substantive equality is because *adversarial relations*— endemic to the antagonistically divided and structurally entrenched capital system of domination and subordination, assuming particularly destructive forms in our time—cannot be overcome in a lasting way without it. The *formal* devices of even the societies with the longest and most broadly diffused democratic traditions could achieve virtually nothing in this respect. On the contrary, in recent times, they have moved in the opposite direction, with a gravely authoritarian curtailment of even the most basic constitutional and civil liberties on a growing scale. Evidently, the relationship not only between humanity and nature but also between states and nations, as well as among particular individuals, must be *mediated* in all conceivable forms of society. Perilously for the future of humankind, the capital system is incapable of operating in any other way than through the imposition—by the most violent means, including potentially catastrophic world wars—of *antagonistic forms and modalities of mediation* (through the hierarchical and discriminatory class structure and through the force exercised by the capitalist state). Only on the basis of substantive equality is it possible to envisage the necessary *non-antagonistic* forms of mediation among human beings at all levels, in a historically sustainable way. It is also important to press, in this context, that what is at stake is not a question of abstract social determinations, capable of being imposed from above in the manner of the inherited forms of authoritarian decision-making typical of capital's mode of social metabolic control. Since the decisions taken directly affect the life of *every particular individual,* non-antagonistic mediation, through active participation in the vital material productive, political, and cultural domain, is conceivable only on a meaningfully *consensual* basis. And that, again, underlines the relevance of substantive equality.

(2) The historic challenge concerning the established mode of *production* and *societal reproduction* is clearly manifest in our time in relation to some major issues. In none of them could the underlying problems be conceptualized in generic social terms because they cannot be abstracted from particular social *individuals,* with their *qualitative* needs and motivations. Since going into details on these matters would take far too long, in the

present context it is only possible to briefly enumerate them.[11] We have already seen in this regard one of the key operative principles of the socialist alternative, concerned with *planning* in the proper sense of the term, as opposed to its unviable *post festum* varieties under the now prevailing sociohistoric conditions. It is necessary to add to that vital concern some equally important issues directly connected with a number of socialist-orienting principles that must become deeply rooted in order to supersede capital's wasteful reproductive order with labor's hegemonic alternative.

These concerns can be recognized in the often unrealistically treated relationship between *scarcity* and *abundance,* as well as in the way in which the category of qualitatively defined real human *need* is tendentiously confused with capitalistically convenient *artificial appetites* which can be manipulatively imposed on individuals in the service of commodity production. It is also important to critically examine the criteria of a really sustainable productive *economy.* This is inseparable from the meaningful and absolutely necessary demand for *economizing* (crucial also in relation to the question of overcoming scarcity) and the long-standing socialist advocacy of managing the societal reproduction process in accordance with the qualitative criteria of *disposable time.* This stands in marked contrast to capital's wasteful and irresponsible *self-expansionary* drive, which is blindly pursued no matter how dangerous the consequences of uncontrollable capital-expansion and imposed on society in the name of quasi-mythical "beneficial growth."

Obviously, the successful operation of the required orienting principle of production and distribution in an advanced socialist order—"from each according to their *abilities,* to each according to their *needs"*—is inconceivable without the conscious acceptance and active promotion of substantive equality by social individuals. But it should be equally clear that the *qualitative* definition and operation of *disposable time*—the potential source of the real (and not narrowly commodified) wealth of both the new social order in general and of "rich social individuals" in the Marxian sense—has a dual sense. On the one hand, it means the total disposable time of society as a whole, rationally planned and allocated to chosen purposes, instead of being dictated by the crude economic determinations of capital's exploitative pursuit of profitable minimal time. But the other sense of disposable time is no less important. It cannot be even imagined without the fully consensual contribution by the particular individuals of their meaningful life-activity, as discussed in the context of genuine planning. And a necessary condition for turning such potentialities into reality, of which so much else depends for making the alternative order historically sustainable, is again the conscious adoption of substantive equality by all concerned.

(3) Naturally, an alternative order of society cannot be instituted without successfully *negating* capital's deeply entrenched mode of social metabolic reproduction. In that sense, *negation* is an essential part of the socialist enterprise under the prevailing historical circumstances. Indeed, in its immediate concerns it is not simply negation but, inevitably at the same time, *"the negation of the negation."* For the social adversary asserts its rule in the form of negating not only the actuality but also even the most remote possibility of human emancipation. This is why the immediate task must be defined in socialist literature as the negation of the negation.

However, such a negative definition of the socialist challenge is unable to fulfill the historic mandate in question, because it remains *in dependency* with what it tries to negate. In order to succeed in the envisaged historic sense, the socialist approach must define itself in *inherently positive* terms. Marx made this absolutely clear when he insisted that: "Socialism is man's *positive self-consciousness,* no longer mediated through the annulment of religion, just as *real life* is man's positive reality, no longer mediated through the annulment of private property."[12] A social order, remaining dependent on the object of its negation, no matter how justified in its original historic terms, cannot offer the required scope for the "rich human being," whose richness is said to arise from his meaningful life-activity "as an inner necessity, as *need*": an inherently *positive* determination. The negative definition of the social setting itself in which the individuals must act, on a continuing basis, would necessarily *prejudge* and *contradict*—through its own negativity—the *aims and objectives* which social individuals are expected to *autonomously and freely* set themselves in an *open-ended* historical order. Moreover, in general societal terms, the requirement of the *non-antagonistic mediation* of humanity's relationship with the natural order, as well as the appropriate regulation of the *cooperative* interchanges of the particular social individuals among themselves, cannot be imagined in terms of the negation of the negation. The vital defining characteristic of the only viable mediating modality of the alternative historical order is *self-mediation*. But to postulate self-mediation in a negative way would be a contradiction in terms.

Naturally, on the basis of these important qualifying conditions, it hardly needs adding that the orienting and operative principle of substantive equality is a necessary constituent of *socialism as humanity's "positive self-consciousness."*

(4) The values necessarily inherited from capital's mode of social metabolic control, with its ferocious cultivation of whatever seems in accord with the system's practical imperative of structurally entrenched domination and subordination, are totally inadequate for the realization of the objectives of the socialist order. Once advocated ideals—like liberty, fraternity, and equality—have been completely emptied of their erstwhile content in the course of capital's descending phase of development. All connections with the Enlightenment tradition of the progressive bourgeoisie had to be broken, and references to "liberty" and "democracy" today are cynically used in the service of oppressive, often even the most brutally violent, even if hypocritically packaged, political and military purposes. The deliberate cultivation and diffusion of false consciousness by the ruling ideology—thanks to its virtual monopoly on the means and devices of mass communication, greatly reinforced by the dominant practices of capital's fetishistic productive order—belongs to the same picture.

Understandably, therefore, the radical alternative, the new historical order, must be consistently articulated also in the domain of values. One of the principal requirements in this respect is that all of the advocated values, not only equality, have to emerge from actually unfolding social practice and be defined in *substantive* terms. It was a major characteristic of the conceptualizations of capital's reproductive order, even in its ascending phase of development, that—due to the system's ineradicable *class* divisions and contradictions—the substantive dimension was pushed into the background and a *formal* definition of positive values was offered in its place.

It is enough to remind ourselves of Kant's treatment of the question of *equality* in this respect.[13] Obviously, the value of *freedom* (or *liberty*) needs as much a substantive determination of its commendable nature in the socialist reproductive order as *equality*. The same goes for *solidarity*, *cooperation,* and *responsibility,* to name only a few of the most important values in labor's hegemonic alternative order. All such concepts, in company with equality and freedom, could be reduced to their formalized skeletons, as they were in fact characteristically transfigured, in as much as they were advocated at all, even in the progressive capitalist past. They acquire legitimacy in the socialist society only if they are adopted as values and orienting principles in their genuine—and most important—substantive sense.

Another vital aspect of this problem is that the value determinations of the socialist order cannot positively prevail unless individual and social consciousness are properly brought together in actual social practice. And that is possible only if the particular social individuals, as freely associated productive individuals, can autonomously realize the values in question in their substantive reality. That is the only way to avoid the danger of "re-establishing 'Society' as an abstraction *vis-à-vis* the individual," to recall Marx's warning.

The categorial reflection of social antagonism from the vantage point of capital was always problematic, and it has become progressively worse with the passing of time. Naturally, there are some powerful reasons for that. Thus, in any attempt to find enduring solutions to these issues, it is necessary to underline the key role of transformative social practice. The dualisms and dichotomies of the post-Cartesian philosophical tradition have arisen from the soil of a determinate social practice, burdened with its insoluble problems. They were representative conceptualizations of deeply rooted *practical antinomies.* To think of theoretically resolving them, simply by means of the adoption of a different categorial framework, would be quite unreal. It is true, of course, that revolutionary practice is unthinkable without the contribution of revolutionary theory. Nevertheless, the dialectical primacy belongs to emancipatory practice itself. One cannot anticipate the solution of the difficult and in so many ways intertwined problems discussed in this chapter in any other way. Without envisaging, that is, the institution of an alternative social order from which the *practical antinomies and contradictions* of capital's mode of societal reproduction are effectively removed.

CHAPTER SEVEN

A Structural Crisis of the System: January 2009 Interview in *Socialist Review*[1]

SR: The ruling class is always surprised by new economic crises and talks about them as aberrations. Why do you believe they are inherent in capitalism?

IM: I recently heard Edmund Phelps, who got the 2006 Nobel Prize in Economics. Phelps is a kind of neo-Keynesian. He was, of course, glorifying capitalism and presenting the current problems as just a little hiccup, saying: "All we have to do now is bring back Keynesian ideas and regulation."

John Maynard Keynes believed that capitalism was ideal, but he wanted regulation. Phelps was churning out the grotesque idea that the system is like a music composer. He may have some off days when he can't produce so well, but if you look at his whole life he's wonderful! Just think of Mozart—he must have had the odd bad day. So that's capitalism in trouble, Mozart's bad days. If anyone believes that, he should have his head examined. But instead of having his head examined he is awarded a prize.

If our adversaries have this level of thought—which they have demonstrated now over a fifty-year period, so it's not just an accidental slip by one award-winning economist—we could say:

"Rejoice, this is the low level of our adversary." But with this kind of conception, you end up with the disaster we experience every day. We have sunk into astronomic debt. The real liabilities in this country must be counted in trillions.

But the important point is that they have been practicing financial profligacy as a result of the structural crisis of the productive system. It is not an accident that money has been flowing in such an adventurist way into the financial sector. The accumulation of capital couldn't function properly in the field of the productive economy.

We are now talking about the structural crisis of the system. It extends everywhere and it even encroaches on our relationship to nature, undermining the fundamental conditions for human survival. For example, from time to time they announce some targets to cut pollution. We even have a ministry of energy and climate change, which is really a ministry of hot air because nothing is done except announcing a target. But the target is never even approached, let alone fulfilled. This is an integral part of the structural crisis of the system and only structural solutions can get us out of this terrible situation.

SR: You have described the United States as carrying out credit card imperialism. What do you mean by that?

IM: I am quoting former senator George McGovern on the Vietnam War. He said that the United States had run the Vietnam War on a credit card. The recent borrowing by the United States is going sour now. This kind of economics can go on only as long as the rest of the world can carry the debt.

The United States is in a unique position because it has been the dominant country since the Bretton Woods agreement. It is a fantasy that a neo-Keynesian solution and a new Bretton Woods would solve any of today's problems. The U.S. domination which Bretton Woods formalized immediately after the Second World War was economically realistic. The U.S. economy was in a much more powerful position than any other economy in the world. It established all the vital international economic institutions on the basis of U.S. privilege—the privilege of the dollar, the privilege enjoyed through the International Monetary Fund, the trade organizations, the World Bank, all of which were completely under U.S. domination and still remain so today.

This cannot be wished out of existence. You can't fantasize about reforming and slightly regulating it here and there. To imagine that Barack Obama is going to abandon the dominant position the United States enjoys in this way—backed up by military domination—is a mistake.

SR: Karl Marx called the ruling class a "band of warring brothers." Do you think the ruling class, internationally, will work together to find a solution?

IM: In the past, imperialism involved several dominant actors who asserted their interests even at the expense of two horrendous world wars in the twentieth century. Partial wars, no matter how horrendous they are, cannot be compared to the economic and power realignment which could be produced by a new world war.

But imagining a new world war is impossible. Of course there are still some lunatics in the military field who would not deny that possibility. But it would mean the total destruction of humanity.

We have to think about the implications of this for the capitalist system. It was a fundamental law of the system that if a force could not be asserted through economic domination you resorted to war.

Global hegemonic imperialism has been achieved and has operated quite successfully since the Second World War. But is that kind of system permanent? Is it conceivable that in the future no contradictions will arise in it?

There have also been some hints from China that this kind of economic domination cannot go on indefinitely. China is not going to be able to go on financing it. The implications and consequences for China are already quite significant. Deng Xiaoping once remarked that the color of the cat—whether it's capitalist or socialist—doesn't matter so long as it catches the mouse. But what if, instead of happy mouse catching, you end up with a horrendous rat infestation in the form of massive unemployment? This is now emerging in China.

These things are inherent in the contradictions and antagonisms of the capitalist system. Therefore, we must think about solving them in a radically different way, and the only way is a genuine socialist transformation of the system.

SR: Is there no decoupling of any part of the world economy from this situation?

IM: Impossible! Globalization is a necessary condition of human development. Ever since the expansion of the capitalist system was clearly visible, Marx theorized this. Martin Wolf of the *Financial Times* has complained that there are too many little, insignificant states that cause trouble. He argued that what is needed is "jurisdictional integration," in other words complete imperialist integration—a fantasy concept. This is an expression of the insoluble contradictions and antagonisms of capitalist globalization. Globalization is a necessity but the form that is feasible, workable, and sustainable is a socialist globalization on the basis of socialist principles of substantive equality.

Although no decoupling from world history is conceivable, it doesn't mean that at every phase, in every part of the world, there is uniformity. Very different things are unfolding in Latin America compared to Europe, not to mention what I have already hinted at in China and the Far East, and Japan, which is in the deepest of trouble.

Just think back a little bit. How many miracles have we had in the postwar period? The German miracle, the Brazilian miracle, the Japanese miracle, the miracle of the five little tigers? How amusing that all these miracles turn into the most awful, prosaic reality. The common denominator of all these realities is disastrous indebtedness and fraud.

One hedge-fund manager has allegedly been involved in a $50 billion swindle. General Motors and the others were only asking the U.S. government for $14 billion. How modest! They should be given $100 billion. If one hedge-fund capitalist can organize an alleged $50 billion fraud, they should get all the funds feasible.

A system that operates in this morally rotten way cannot possibly survive, because it is uncontrollable. People are even admitting that they don't know how it works. The solution is not to despair about it but to control it in the interests of social responsibility and a radical transformation of society.

SR: The drive inherent in capitalism is to squeeze workers as hard as possible, and that's clearly what governments are trying to do in Britain and the United States.

IM: The only thing they can do is advocate cutting workers' wages. The principal reason why the Senate refused to pass even the $14 billion injection into the big three U.S. car companies is they could not get agreement on a drastic reduction of workers' wages. Think about the effect of that and the kind of obligations those workers have—for instance repaying massive mortgages. To ask them simply to halve their wages would generate other problems in the economy—again a contradiction.

Capital and contradictions are inseparable. We have to go beyond the superficial manifestations of those contradictions to their roots. You manage to manipulate them here and there but they will come back with a vengeance. Contradictions cannot be shoved under the carpet indefinitely because the carpet is now becoming a mountain.

SR: You studied with Georg Lukács, a Marxist who goes back to the period of the Russian Revolution.

IM: I worked with Lukács for seven years before I left Hungary in 1956, and we remained very close friends until he died in 1971. We always saw eye to eye—that's why I wanted to study with him. It so happened that when I arrived to work with him he was being attacked very fiercely and openly in public. I could not stomach that and defended him, which led to all sorts of complications. Just as I left Hungary, I was designated by Lukács as his successor at the university, teaching his course on aesthetics. The reason I left was precisely because I was convinced that what was going on was a variety of very fundamental problems, which that system could not resolve.

I tried to formulate and examine these problems in my books since then, in particular in *Marx's Theory of Alienation* and *Beyond*

Capital. Lukács used to say, quite rightly, that without strategy you can't have tactics. Without a strategic view of these problems you cannot have the everyday solutions. So I have tried to analyze these problems consistently because they cannot be simply treated at the level of an article that relates only to what is happening today, though there is a big temptation to do that. Instead, it has to be done within a historical perspective. My first fairly substantial essay was published in 1950, in a literary periodical in Hungary, and I have been working as hard as I could ever since. In whatever modest way we can, we make our contribution towards change. That's what I have tried to do all my life.

SR: What do you think the possibilities for change are at the moment?

IM: Socialists are the last to minimize the difficulties of the solution. Capital apologists, whether they are neo-Keynesian or whatever else, can produce all kinds of simplistic solutions. I don't think that we can consider the present crisis simply in the way we have in the past. The present crisis is profound. The deputy governor of the Bank of England has admitted that this is the greatest economic crisis in human history. I would only add that it is not the greatest economic crisis in human history but the greatest crisis in all senses. Economic crises cannot be separated from the rest of the system.

The fraudulence and domination of capital and the exploitation of the working class cannot go on forever. The producers cannot be kept constantly and forever under control. Marx argued that capitalists are simply the personifications of capital. They are not free agents; they are executing the imperatives of this system. So the problem for humanity is not simply to sweep away one bunch of capitalists. To simply put one type of personification of capital in the place of another would lead to the same disaster, and sooner or later we'd end up with the restoration of capitalism.

The problems society faces have not simply arisen in the past few years. Sooner or later these have to be resolved, and not, as the Nobel Prize–winning economists might fantasize, within the framework of the system. The only possible solution is to found social reproduction on the basis of the producers being in control. That has always been the idea of socialism.

We have reached the historical limits of capital's ability to control society. I don't mean just banks and building societies, even though they cannot control those, but the rest. When things go wrong nobody's responsible. From time to time politicians say, "I accept full responsibility," and what happens? They are glorified. The only feasible alternative is the working class, the producer of everything necessary in our life. Why should the working class not be in control of what they produce? I always stress in every book that saying no is relatively easy, but we have to find the positive dimension.

CHAPTER EIGHT

The Tasks Ahead: March 2009
Interview in *Debate Socialista*

1. THE GLOBAL EXPLOSION OF CAPITAL'S STRUCTURAL CRISIS

DS: In *Beyond Capital*, you analyze the continuous deepening of capital's structural crisis and the related possibility of humanity's destruction. Does the present global economic crisis signal a qualitative change in this direction?

IM: The currently unfolding crisis is certainly very grave and in an important sense different from that of the last few decades. To be sure, it remains the same *structural* crisis which we have experienced since the end of the 1960s or the beginning of the 1970s, but it is different in the sense that now the crisis has *globally erupted into the open with great vehemence.* I was always convinced that the May events in France in 1968 were an integral part of the necessary onset of such structural crisis. At the end of 1967—in a conversation with my dear friend Lucien Goldman, who in those days still believed, like Marcuse, that "organized capitalism" had succeeded in solving the problems of "crisis capitalism"—I expressed my conviction that the gravest of crises was ahead of us. For so-called organized capitalism solved no crisis at all. On the contrary, I argued at the time, the crisis we were heading for would have to be incomparably more severe than even the Great World Economic Crisis of 1929–1933, in view of its truly global character. It would have to be global, I have insisted ever since, in the real sense of the term for the first time ever in history.

I have sharply contrasted the epochal *structural crisis* of the capital system, prevailing in our time, with the *cyclic* and *conjunctural* economic crises of the past. The periodically occurring *cyclic* crises will remain a prominent feature of *capitalist conjunctural development* for as long as capitalism survives. But in our own historical epoch there is a much more fundamental type of crisis, combined with cyclic crises under capitalism, affecting *all conceivable forms of the capital system as such,* not only capitalism. Structural crisis asserts itself in the form of *activating the absolute limits of capital as a mode of social metabolic reproduction.* This is why the Soviet-type capital system—which should not be confused with the *primarily economic* extraction of surplus-labor as *surplus-value* under capitalism, since it operated on the basis of the *overwhelmingly political* extraction of *surplus-labor*—had to implode under the globally intensifying contradictions of development. This must be emphasized today as firmly as possible. Precisely in order to avoid some of the most painful illusions and corresponding blind alleys of the past while facing the great challenges of our future.

In *Beyond Capital*, I wrote that the "*mode* of unfolding" of the structural crisis "might be called *creeping*—in contrast to the more spectacular and dramatic eruptions and collapses of the past— while adding the proviso that even the most vehement or violent convulsions cannot be excluded as far as the future is concerned: i.e., when the complex machinery now actively engaged in 'crisis management' and in the more or less temporary 'displacement' of the growing contradictions runs out of steam."[1] The dramatic manifestations of our present crisis—from the multiplication of so-called *wildcat strikes* in the capitalistically most advanced parts of the world to *food riots* in more than thirty-five countries, reported by no less an establishment authority than *The Economist*—indicate that great masses of people, gravely affected by what is no longer a readily manipulable *financial* crisis, may strongly refute the self-complacent and capital-apologetic wisdom of the recent past. Working people, trapped within the limits of their defensive organizations—strictly wage-oriented and reformist trade unions and parties—were expected to behave like purring pussy cats and not like *wildcats*. The so-called wildcat strikes (and associated solidarity strikes) were outlawed in Britain by savage Thatcherite legislation. Revealingly, such anti-union laws were not only retained (despite some pre-election promises to the contrary) but made even worse by the New Labour government.

Thus, the present crisis is different in the sense that it is beginning to produce defiant and radical responses on a considerable scale. And this process is very far from having reached its climax. At the same time, the measures adopted with dubious results by the dominant capitalist governments—amounting to the *nationalization of capitalist bankruptcy* through the mind-boggling expenditure of *trillions of dollars*—are also clear evidence that nothing could be more foolish than to describe the present crisis as yet another traditional cyclic crisis of capitalism, which is to be swept out of the way in a year or two, as the "hired prize fighters of capital" (in Marx's words) continue to characterize it even today.

The gravely unfolding crisis of our historical epoch is *structural*, precisely in the sense that it cannot be swept out of the way even by the many *trillions* of dollars spent in state capitalist rescue operations. Thus, the deepening structural crisis of the system, together with the demonstrable failure of the attempted remedial measures, in the form of military and financial adventurism on a formerly unimaginable scale, make the danger of humanity's self-destruction greater than ever before. For such dangers can only multiply when the traditional forms and instruments of control at the disposal of the established order fail to do their job. It is not surprising, therefore, that the dominant imperialist power today, the United States, openly claims the "moral right" to use nuclear weapons whenever it so decides, even against non-nuclear countries.

2. IN PLACE OF NEO-KEYNESIAN ILLUSIONS: THE STRATEGIC OFFENSIVE OF ANTI-SYSTEMIC FORCES

DS: Is a capitalist solution for this crisis (with such neo-Keynesian measures as regulation and protectionism) possible? What is your opinion about the claims of some government leaders (like Lula in Brazil) that it is possible to keep some countries decoupled from the turmoil?

IM: One of the understandable, but ultimately self-defeating, illusions we have to guard against is any form of *neo-Keynesianism,* including so-called *left-Keynesianism.* The calls for its revival today are understandable because they correspond to *the line of least resistance* to which the personifications of capital can *temporarily* agree under the circumstances of a major crisis. Under such circumstances, the personifications of capital are willing to use Keynesian state-interventionist measures for the *restabilization of their system,* and to do so until they can fully reverse their *concessions* and return to the *status quo ante.*

Leading spokesmen of capital are now openly calling for the *nationalization of some major banks,* and they are also engaged in the implementation of that proposal in a form suitable to their interest. Indeed, they have instituted in Britain recently a most hypocritical form of "nationalization" of nearly all of the major (totally bankrupt) banks. The spokesmen of capital have unabashedly added at the same time that "in due course the publicly recapitalized banks will be returned to the private sector again." This they can openly say because they have nationalized capitalist bankruptcy before (immediately after the Second World War in Britain on a major scale) and re-privatized all of the principal units of postwar nationalization after properly fattening them up from the generous resources of the public purse. And they are confident that they can do the same trick again when the crisis dies down.

To be sure, the spokesmen of capital are not entirely mistaken in their pro-Keynesian disposition. This is because it depends primarily on the organizations of the working class whether or not this kind of approach can in the end prevail. For even a major historic crisis cannot spontaneously accomplish the difficult task of the required, strategically viable and combative organized action of the labor movement. The present situation is by no means unique in that respect. Historically promising opportunities for a much needed radical transformation not only arise from time to time but can also be missed.[2]

We live in a historical period of fundamental structural crisis, which may open up a *sizeable breach in the established order* because that order is no longer capable of delivering the goods that served as its—unquestioned—justification in the past. Also today, applying neo-Keynesian remedies to the now unfolding crisis could only fill in the breach, temporarily revitalizing capital in the interest of its continued survival, as happened in the postwar period of Keynesian capital-expansion. This is bound to be the case, no matter how subjectively well-meaning some of the people might be who—in contrast to capital's cynically calculating state-interventionist personifications—continue to advocate the formerly tried, and from the standpoint of the working class conclusively failed, left-Keynesian policies of redistributive social reform.

Revealingly, under the present circumstances of capital's dramatically unfolding crisis, workers are induced—by their own trade union representatives in Britain—not to mention "their" New Labour Party—to agree to tightening their belts and to accepting necessary sacrifices, including not only a *wage freeze for two years* but even significant *wage-cuts*—in the interest of *re-stabilizing* the system. All of this comes with a vacuous promise of some improvement in the "post-crisis" future. In the spirit of this defensive line of Labourite approach, the opportunities for instituting strategically viable change are always missed, with reference to the force of circumstance. Everything is left, at best, to a generically hoped for future, which can never come if the tangible opportunities of even a monumental social and economic crisis are missed as a matter of course, thanks to the adopted accommodation.

In truth, the vainly postulated redistributive reforms (including their left-Keynesian varieties) never did—and *never could*—work within the structurally entrenched confines of the capital system. So much has been repeatedly promised in this respect and nothing ever maintained. As a result, even one of the staunchest apologists of the established order, Martin Wolf, the Associate Editor of the London-based *Financial Times,* had to admit that the inequality between the richest and the poorest countries of the world dramatically increased in the period of capitalist modernization and globalization. "Today that ratio is some *seventy five to one.* A century ago, it was about *ten to one.* In half a century, it could all too easily be *one hundred and fifty to one.*"[3] And this century of increase in inequality actually took place on a staggering scale, despite the endlessly repeated promises of moving in the direction of its elimination, or at least significant reduction. This century included *eighty years of Keynesian advocacy* of major remedial action. For the plain truth of the matter is, in contrast to neo-Keynesian fantasies, that we need *fundamental structural change*—and not the reformist repositioning of the recliner chairs on the top deck of the Titanic.

For the same reason, the prospect of unavoidable failure in the absence of a real structural change, I am no less skeptical about the idea of "delinking" than about past or present Keynesianism. We cannot seriously believe that the cry—"stop the world, I want to get off"—can produce the required solution. Capitalist globalization, no matter how pernicious it happens to be, is both the *actuality* and the objective *necessity* of the capital system's historical development, inseparable from its innermost *structural determinations* as a long established mode of social reproductive control. Marx and Engels way back in 1848, in the *Communist Manifesto,* highlighted the dynamic tendency of this system for global encroachment.

Thus, delinking could at best work only as a *temporary defensive measure,* even in the case of a continent-size country like Brazil. The grave problem facing us at the present juncture of history is not the objective tendency to humanity's global economic integration but the antagonistic and ever more *destructive* character of *monopolist and imperialist globalization.* Only that kind of globalization is appropriate to the *capital system.* This means that what is at stake under the present conditions of capital's grave structural crisis is not simply a way of devising some defensive and protective measures against the *financial* domination of the principal *capitalist* countries. That could amount only to a rather naïve defensiveness, which would be expected to offer some limited regulatory safeguard against criticized *excesses* while remaining within the same operational framework of the established order. It could not be successful because, sooner or later, an unavoidable challenge must be faced: the issue is the radical transformation of the *incorrigible systemic determinations* of capital as a mode of ultimately self-destructive societal control. Accordingly, even if the operation of a delinked domain proved feasible at all, it would before long suffer the same fate as the rest of the world in the absence of fundamental *systemic change*.

Naturally, the *regional* combination of the *anti-systemic* forces of Latin America is a very different matter. It can be advocated with legitimacy and pursued with uncompromising determination. But such a strategy could not be described in terms of the unsustainable and defensive project of delinking. For its success or failure would depend precisely on its ability to militantly counter the destructive course of action necessarily arising from capital's systemic determinations. In that way, the strategy in question would have to go well beyond challenging the limits of the global capitalist *financial* system, which has been dominated for a very long time by the United States in support of its astronomic and ever-escalating debt.

3. MONOPOLISTIC ECONOMY AND CREDIT CARD IMPERIALISM

DS: You have said recently that the United States is carrying out credit-card imperialism. What do you mean by that? What economic and political changes, in your view, will emerge in the global imperialist configuration after this crisis?

IM: The credit-card imperialism of the United States is not new. Senator McGovern criticized it, at the time of the Vietnam War, saying that: "we have been waging that war on a credit card." The difference today is that the sums involved, on the inexorably growing debit side of U.S.-credit-card imperialism, are truly astronomical. And despite all that, the imperialist wars of the United States continue to be waged unabated, ignoring the fact that such wars can not be economically sustained without the rest of the world paying for them, including—in a most ironical sense and no doubt making Mao Tse-Tung turn in his grave—present-day China. The latter alone is doing it to the tune of well over $1 trillion.

President Obama recently announced that he is going to *reduce by 50 percent* the *$1.3 trillion* annual U.S. budgetary deficit during the four years of his first presidential term. And, curiously, he asked Congress, at the same time he committed to the 50 percent reduction, to approve for the first year of his current term a *deficit of $1.7 trillion* Isn't that a great start for the fulfillment of Obama's presidential promise? Especially in view of the fact that the budgetary deficit of the U.S. Government is only *one* of the *three* chronic dimensions of the—hard even to imagine—American debt, in addition to massive *corporate* as well as *individual* indebtedness!

Also it is clearly visible that we are gravely burdened with some fundamental *systemic problems*, which cannot be solved within the confines of the *capital system*. For imperialism is not simply a question of capitalist *political inter-state relations*—together with the associated wars—which could be left behind by humanity thanks to the *good will* of some *enlightened politicians*. On the contrary, the now dominant form of global hegemonic imperialism is an objective *systemic necessity of capital* in our epoch of historical development. Thus, it is absolutely *incorrigible* within the framework of the capital system as such. The fact that we are not at present involved in yet another *world war* is due to the equally incorrigible circumstance that such a war would destroy humanity itself, leaving the planet fit only for cockroaches.

But no one should consider the avoidance of a devastating global war under globalized capitalism a *certainty*, if we do not remove the deep-seated *systemic causes* for the eventuality of such a war. As a matter of historical record, humanity has never invented any destructive machinery which it has not used in anger on a scale commensurate to its potential. In fact, openly war-mongering talk in U.S. military circles, together with the associated government decrees about the necessity—and also the claimed moral right—for using nuclear weapons continues unabated. So too does the refusal to abandon the purported right to a first strike, even against non-nuclear powers, *preemptively* and not just *preventively*, despite the public appeal of eighteen hundred concerned American scientists, including a good number of Nobel Prize winners, addressed to the Bush Administration in the autumn of 2005.[4] And President Obama has made no declaration to the contrary. Indeed, his Secretary of State, Hillary Clinton, declared during her campaign for presidential candidacy, that she would not recoil from using nuclear weapons against Iran. Moreover, a decade or so earlier, in the most aggressive U.S. military circles not simply Iran but China was indicated as the future target of a necessary war, to be waged with the appropriate weaponry, which of course could not be anything but nuclear. Likewise, as Pakistan's General Musharraf revealed in a U.S. television interview in Washington, he was threatened by the former Deputy Secretary of State, Richard Armitage, who said to him that Pakistan would be *bombed back to the stone age* if his government refused to obey American orders. This is a threat whose realization would be quite impossible in a big country like Pakistan without the use of nuclear weapons.

It is important to underline here that the potentially deadliest form of global hegemonic imperialism, ruthlessly asserting itself in our time, is inseparable on the material reproductive plane from the present historical phase of *monopolistic economic development* and the *centralization of power* corresponding to it. This inseparability of the two dimensions highlights again that the explosive antagonisms are *systemic* and can be overcome only through the radical change of the capital system itself. Accordingly, some of the worst *manifestations* of the global financial crisis may be diminished, or even temporarily brought under control, but not the *structural crisis itself*. That is bound to remain with us, and erupt again and again in a more or less dramatic form, for as long as the fundamental *structural determinations* of the capital system are not radically changed.

Thus, we can refer to the condition *"after the crisis"* only in a very limited sense. For the *inherent antagonisms* of the monopolistic economic system under U.S. domination—with worsening levels of *destructive production* which directly endanger even the nature-dependent conditions of human survival in our planetary household—will assert themselves as before, despite all *governmental hot-air generation* to the contrary (now described as the "green industrial revolution"). Also, the *material ground* of global hegemonic imperialist political and military adventurism is not going to evaporate through the force of even the most eloquent presidential rhetoric.

It should not be forgotten that the disastrous state of the global financial system is as much the manifestation of the present phase of development of both monopoly and imperialism as the wars pursued today—and yet to come—with immense material waste and boundless human sacrifices at the receiving end. No one denies the prominence of the United States in its imperialist wars, even if both in Iraq and in Afghanistan they are "modestly" described by the propagandists of the ruling order as only "U.S.-*led*"—rather than U.S.-*imposed*—wars (imposed, that is, also on the so-called willing allies). They clearly manifest the currently attained level of *centralization of power* in the political and military domain of inter-state relations. However, it is conveniently disregarded, because of the complicitous subservience of the "willing allies," who claim to be "sovereign democratic countries of the free world," that in the global economic and financial domain the same kind of *centralization of power* prevails. This is as clearly demonstrated by the *international chain-reaction* caused by the U.S. mortgage and banking collapse as in the political and military domain. And that relationship corresponds to the same overall U.S. dominance at the present historic phase of monopolistic economic developments on a global scale. President Clinton's deputy Secretary of State, Strobe Talbot, made it brutally clear at a meeting held in London that the move toward greater European unity is acceptable to the United States only *"so long as it does not threaten U.S. global pre-eminence."*[5]

In view of their structurally determined inseparability and *reciprocally reinforcing power*, both monopoly and imperialism must be consigned to the past, as the incorrigible characteristics of the *capital system as such* at its contemporary phase of development, if humanity is to survive. Only in that case may we talk in a full sense about the advocated and hoped for condition of *"after the crisis."*

4. THE IRRATIONALITY OF CAPITALIST "DOWNSIZING" IN THE AGE OF "MONOPOLY-FINANCE CAPITAL"

DS: During the nineties, we saw a part of the leftist intelligentsia and a part of the militant left adopting the view that the role of the working class was over and even labor was not central any longer in a global analysis. What do you think about this view? Does not the present crisis, with its massive job cuts, deny it in some way?

IM: Saying "farewell to the working class" is fundamentally wrong, whatever might be the motivations behind it. The accommodating version of such a view is based on a total misconception of labor and its role in socialist strategy. It tends to identify the concept of the working class with *manual workers,* falsely concluding from its own false premise that—in view of the undeniable technological developments characteristic of "advanced capitalism"—the working class loses its relevance in social transformation, thereby "refuting" Marx's theory.

However, even the assertion about the great diminution of the class of manual workers is quite wrong if considered in its *global* setting, instead of blindly confined to advanced capitalism. In the last fifty years, the overall number of manual workers has significantly *increased* in the labor force—through the, criminally cost-cutting and even in elementary safety measures cynically economizing, transfer of the smoke-stack industries to the so-called Third World, producing catastrophic accidents like the one witnessed at Bhopal in India.

However, the centrally important issue in this whole matter is quite different. It concerns not the various *sociological strata* which make up the totality of the working class, both internally in any particular country and internationally in capital's global order, but the *overall force* of *labor*—that is, in strategically vital theoretical terms, its general category—as *the only feasible hegemonic alternative to capital's mode of societal reproduction.* The ever more destructive *logic of capital,* which rules with absolute authoritarianism our entire system of *social metabolic reproduction,* must be (and can only be effectively) opposed in *global* terms, embracing all aspects of human life. This demands the productively viable and historically sustainable *emancipatory and self-emancipatory logic of labor,* instituted by the *totality of labor* and not by any particular section or sociological strata of labor.

Marx in his time was talking about the irresistibly unfolding *proletarianization* (not manual-laborization) taking place in capitalist society. Such proletarianization affects all categories of the labor force, resulting in the *loss of control* even over the most limited aspects of life which individuals once may have had in some "white collar" and "service" branches of activity. This loss of control is unmistakably evidenced in twentieth century developments, as demonstrated by the *total insecurity* dominating all kinds of working people in our own time. Marx contrasted such *alienating proletarianization* with the powers arising from labor's self-emancipatory logic, extended to all members of society in their capacity as *substantively equal* and genuine *decision-makers* over all vital issues of life. This stands in marked contrast to the pseudo-democratic practice of legitimating capital's authoritarianism in the workshop and tyranny in the market by throwing once in four or five years a piece of paper into the ballot box. The successful institution and positively oriented constant development of this *hegemonic alternative* of labor to capital's incurably iniquitous order remains the fundamental strategic orienting principle for us also in our own historical epoch of development. The claim that "there is no alternative" to capital's societal reproductive order imposes the kind of devastating uncontrollability and destructiveness which we are experiencing today under the circumstances of our global socioeconomic crisis.

At the beginning of March 2009, it was made public that in the United States the number of the unemployed had increased in the

month of February alone by *651,000*: a staggering figure by any
standard. Curiously, the stock exchanges received the news with a
sigh of relief. Even more curiously, the *ex officio* apologists of the
system—both financial and political—commented that this (temporarily improved and soon afterwards reversed) stock exchange
result was proof that the *recession is bottoming out,* and thus we can
see the green shoots of revival appearing again. The claimed proof
was in fact nothing of the kind. Instead, the brief stock exchange rise
was a mindless reaction—a sort of capitalist Pavlovian reflex—in
tune with the callous and degrading wisdom which greets the ejec-
tion of the masses of the people from the labor process as the welcome sign of *"downsizing"* and a corresponding improvement in
profitability.

The apologists in question did not seem to notice that: (1) a
monthly *downsizing of 651,000 people* in the United States might
not be sustainable for a long time, even under the best of global economic circumstances; and (2) that we are not living right now under
the best of global economic circumstances at all, but under those of
an unprecedented *global economic crisis.* Moreover, *downsizing* as a
general rule is an absurd strategy for the capital system as a whole.
For it is sustainable only as the *exception* enforced for some time by
the *more powerful* units of capital over against the *weaker* ones, but
it is totally unviable for securing the health of the system in its
entirety. It is *self-contradictory* as a matter of *inner systemic determinations.* This is well in keeping with the nature of capital as a societal reproductive order of *insoluble contradictions.* Capital needs the
workers not only for the purpose of *profitable production* but also as
profit-producing consumers. Downsizing generalized, as an overall
"rationalizing" panacea is quite *irrational.* If it was extended over
the labor force as a whole, it would result in the *implosion of capitalism* itself, as a result of totally failed capital-accumulation, due to
the absence of profitable production that can only be realized on the
necessary extended scale through profit-producing mass consumption. The world of adventurist financial speculation and the near-
astronomic remuneration of bankers, recently highlighted in the
scandals of the global financial crisis, cannot provide an even

remotely sustainable alternative purchasing power to the now brutally downsized labor force.

Financial journalists suddenly started to use the expression—"the real economy"—with remarkable frequency. Earlier they proclaimed that the most important part of the modern economy was the courageously risk-taking financial sector, which seemed to be able to produce unlimited capital-expansion. And, of course, no remuneration could be considered too high for such courageous risk-taking, even if the capital-expansion produced in that way, through adventurist financial speculation and uncontrollable banking "excesses," was largely *fictitious*, if not utterly *fraudulent*. It was greatly facilitated by the corrupt *symbiotic* relationship, between the financial system itself and the legal jungle produced by the capitalist state, suitable to the requirements of speculative adventurist finance capital.

Now, suddenly, the concept of the "real economy" has become palatable again, without however identifying the *causal connection* between the disaster created in the global financial system and the totally irresponsible relegation of *real productive labor* to a domain which must be endlessly *down-sized* in the books of proper "economic science" and, thus, *cut to the bone*. The devastating speculative adventurism in the world of finance, in our age of "monopoly-finance capital,"[6] is to a most significant extent due to the failure of sufficient capital-accumulation in the *productive field* and the concomitant transfer of capital into the adventurist-speculative financial sector. Here, a *single* capitalist—Bernie Madoff, the former head of NASDAQ—could fraudulently appropriate the immense sum of *$65 billion*.[7] Now the chicken are coming home to roost, as the saying goes, as a result of the sharp contradiction between *real productive activity* and *parasitic finance*.

The gravity of the present crisis is underlined by the fact that no solution can be envisaged to the present global crisis without substantively remedying—on a lasting basis and not by the unendurable *bailout* of capitalist bankruptcy in banking and insurance—capital's flight from the *productive domain*, due to the chronic failure of capital-accumulation in that field on the required scale. A failure dramatically highlighted recently also by the near (and potentially total) bankruptcy of the giant American automobile companies, from Ford to General Motors and Chrysler. Thus, *productive labor*, at our own stage of historical development, is of greater importance than ever before, no matter how hard the personifications of capital and their hired prize fighters might try to deny it in the name of advanced capitalism.

5. DEEP-SEATED SYSTEMIC PROBLEMS CALL FOR STRUCTURAL REMEDIES

DS: What is your evaluation of the alternatives to capital considered in the 1990s? And nowadays? Does the present crisis open new possibilities for the working class and the socialist project?

IM: Prime Minister Margaret Thatcher popularized the arrogant slogan that *"there is no alternative"* to the aggressive neoliberal and monetarist variety of capital's rule. She also boasted—after the defeat of the year-long strike of the British miners, facilitated by state repression and the active complicity of Neil Kinnock's Labour Party—that she had *"seen off socialism for good."* Thatcher's self-delusion seemed to have been confirmed not only by the way in which she could "do business with Mr. Gorbachev," as she put it in praise of the Soviet President and Party Secretary, but also by the transformation of the British Labour Party into Tony Blair's New Labour.

Already the 1980s marked the success of aggressive—and socially regressive—neoliberalism all over the world. Today, rather one-sidedly, many commentators indicate *deregulation* as the cause of the global financial troubles, postulating at the same time the superficial remedy of devising a global financial regulatory system. However, they avoid a highly embarrassing question: why did the wholesale deregulation of the global financial system, under American domination, come into being in the first place? And, moreover, what are the chances of success for the vaguely projected regulatory system if the powerful structural determinations at the roots of the now criticized system—which are never even mentioned—are not radically altered in a causally sustainable way?

Deregulation in Britain—a country once at the forefront of the world's Industrial Revolution, but more recently a kingdom whose financial sector has been grotesquely inflated and now (at least for the time being) rather deflated—went hand in hand with a frightening degree of *deindustrialization* in the 1980s and 1990s. Under those circumstances the politicians as well as the captains of industry, together with the bankers, dismantled a large proportion of the productive economy, from ship-building to engineering and motor-car production, with the delusory self-justification that in the "value-added modern economy" the service sector and international finance represent the "vanguard of progress." Similar practices were adopted also in other advanced capitalist countries, transferring not only the smokestack industries but also some other branches of labor-intensive productive activity to the super-exploited Third World, with the absurd ideological rationalization that we now live in a post-industrial society.

Sadly, in the decades of the 1980s and 1990s, extended also into the first decade of the twenty first century, the international left on the whole went along with these transformations. This was evidenced not only by the implosion of the Soviet-type system, under Gorbachev, but also by the capitulatory change in perspective adopted by some prominent former Western Maoist figures. And, in terms of the size of electoral representation, most prominently by social democratic and labor parties all over the world. Thus, in a speech made by Tony Blair on April Fool's Day in 1995, the Leader of the New Labour Party—who held the office of Prime Minister in Britain for a whole decade, between 1997–2007—declared that the new party is now "the Party of modern business and industry." Indeed, the Party had abandoned all of its former transformative commitments, evacuating from its constitution Clause 4, which called for the public ownership of the means of production. I wrote at the time, two years before Blair's electoral victory, that in this way the purportedly working class party of New Labour is going to win a Pyrrhic victory, but the question is bound to remain with us: "how long will the class of labor allow itself to be treated like April's Fool and how long can the strategy of capitulating to big business be pursued beyond the *coming Pyrrhic electoral victory?*"[8]

In light of the unfolding and deepening global crisis, only a fool could deny that the strategies of neoliberalism miserably and devastatingly failed. At the same time, of course, the accommodating response of the left also failed. Thus, the answer to the second half of your question can only be: *"it depends."* There can be no doubt that—given the severity of the global crisis and the savagery of the measures that must be adopted by the personifications of capital against the working class in their attempts to solve it, in sharp contrast to the *soothing trillions* invested in rescuing capitalist financial bankruptcy—*new possibilities* are opened to the working class and to those who remained faithful to the socialist project for a radical structural transformation of the established order. However, they are only *possibilities* and by no means *certainties,* despite the unprecedented gravity of the crisis. *It depends* on the ability and determination of committed socialist forces to formulate a comprehensive strategy and to organize themselves accordingly, extending their influence in a radically improved way among the great masses of the people, in the interest of the realization of that strategy.

The only certainty is that the reformist accommodations of the past cannot succeed on a lasting basis. The present crisis is far too deep for that. Only a radical structural transformation, irreversibly affecting the systemic parameters of the established order, can offer a sustainable solution. But despite that, at the time of a major crisis the temptation to opt for *the line of least resistance* is understandable and widespread. Today, the earlier mentioned acceptance of a *wage-freeze* for two years and even significant *wage cuts,* together with the call by trade union and political leaders for *tightening the belt,* point in that direction. Also the relative ease with which massive new measures of downsizing can be imposed on the labor force—for instance, the 651,000 jobs lost in February in the United States—indicate the same problem. The remedial wisdom—loudly trumpeted through the quasi-monopolistically controlled media—talks about (rather fictitious) *regulation,* yet to be established on the ruins of the aggressive deregulations of the past. The temptation to give credence to such "regulatory wisdom" is well in tune with the line of least resistance. However, the crisis-alleviating result of the now promised regulation can only be temporary. Deep-seated structural problems can only be solved by radical structural measures. In that important sense, the socialist forces can rightfully claim today a new opening for their emancipatory vision. But the *possibilities* of this new opening can only be turned into the *actuality* of effective systemic change through the passionately dedicated hard work of strategically pursued organization and education.

6. SECTORIAL INTERESTS AND CLASS SOLIDARITY

DS: In *Socialism or Barbarism*, you emphasize that a new articulation between unions and workers parties should be, in the twenty-first century, completely different from that of the twentieth century. What should be the union's role and the party's role? What are their programmatic tasks to make possible overcoming capital?

IM: Perhaps the most successful guiding tenet of the ruling order in the course of class history, invented by the Romans well before the onset of capitalism, has been and remains: *divide et impera,* (divide and rule). Indeed, damaging divisions in the ranks of the working class are painfully in evidence both internally, in every single country, and internationally, across state barriers.

What makes this problem particularly difficult to overcome is the fact that such divisions do not prevail only in the political domain but characterize society as a whole. This is what really explains why the pernicious tenet of divide and rule has been, on the face of it, amazingly successful throughout countless centuries of class history. If it was not for the deep-seated social ramifications of this problem, the enlightening political persuasion of individuals—who are simply said to be misled by the ruling ideology, as this issue is often characterized in political discourse even on the left—could remedy the situation by itself. By adopting that line of approach, some weighty objective differences of material and cultural interest, together with their manifestations on the institutional and organizational plane, tend to be neglected or even totally disregarded, adding thereby to the problems instead of facilitating their removal.

I have quoted in the past the shocking—but by no means exceptional—figure that in the motor car company of Ford Philippines the assembly line workers received *twenty-five times less* in hourly wages for the *same work* as their social brothers in the Detroit Ford plants. As a more recent example of such massive differences in income, we may recall that some crane operators loading containerized ships on the West Coast of the United States earn annually around *$160,000*, when billions of people in the world must somehow survive (if they do) on *less than two dollars* per day. It would take much more than even the best form of *ideological clarification* to resolve such divisions of interest among the great masses of people who are subordinated to the rule of capital, including their more privileged sections. Growing unemployment in the world today, under the direct impact of the unfolding global crisis, can only underline the severity of this problem. This is a problem which cannot be overcome without the adoption of a radical socialist strategy and the corresponding, organizationally sustainable form of industrial and political action.

The great difficulty in this respect is the paralyzing contradiction between the *immediate* demands and pressures, often legitimate, and the *comprehensive strategic framework* in which they should be pursued. I fully agree with Fernando Silva who wrote recently that:

> *As lutas salariais e ações setoriais são importantes para despertar a consciência da classe, mas, se não estão balizadas por um projeto de poder político, de superação do capital e seu estado, por mais radicais que elas sejam, se esfumam em enormes gastos de energias que em geral podem ser relativamente tolerados e assimilados (ainda que contidos e reprimidos) pelo sistema se não avançam para questionar a ordem, o poder e a propriedade do capital.*[9]

The stratifications in existence have not only historical roots but frequently also additional supporting force in the more or less important role fulfilled by different strata under given circumstances in capital's reproduction process. These complicating objective factors cannot be either ignored or overcome in a short space of time, no matter how desirable it might be to do so. Historical development is characterized by the complex relationship between *continuity and discontinuity*. We ignore that only at our peril.

But acknowledging the dialectical relationship between continuity and discontinuity, which cannot be sidestepped, should not mean that we accommodate ourselves in an unprincipled way to the pressure of the self-perpetuating *immediate*. That would be at the expense of advancing a *strategically necessary comprehensive framework* in which the paralyzing contradictions arising from the most iniquitous stratifications and immediate interests could be resolved in the vital *overall interest* of the realization of labor's *hegemonic alternative* to capital's evermore destructive societal reproductive order. For even the most privileged constituents of the given stratifications are by no means immune to the devastating impact of capital's structural crisis in the long run. The plight of growing unemployment as a result of the global crisis, gravely affecting all categories of labor, speaks loud enough for that.

In our own time, the *defensive* articulation of the working-class movement—characteristic of the twentieth century—cannot be maintained any longer if we want to find historically sustainable solutions to the *deepening crisis of the capital system*. The divisive organizational articulation between the "industrial arm" (the trade unions) and the "political arm" (the various parties) of the working class movement *necessarily* failed to achieve the originally envisaged *overall strategic aim* of the socialist movement. By consenting to confine *industrial action* to limited (and inescapably divisive and stratifying) wage improvements, which meant institutionally and organizationally renouncing the vital need for acquiring control over the material reproductive enterprises themselves, and by limiting *political action* of the working class parties to integrable reformist objectives, which could be contained well within capital's reproductive framework, *both arms* had lost their potential power for qualitative social transformation. Thus, capital's reproductive *imperatives* and corresponding *dictates* could prevail with all of its political pretences to parliamentary democracy.

Such democracy forbids, as an *absolute taboo,* both any engagement in direct political action by the industrial arm and any effort aimed at effectively taking over control of the industrial enterprises on a comprehensive scale by the political arm of the class. As such, it has condemned the labor movement to powerlessness for more than a century. Once *radical control* of the material dimension of societal reproduction is ruled out, as it has been, the power at the disposal of the subordinate class of labor must be strictly *marginal,* confined to extremely limited improvements which have to be integrable (and are actually integrated) within the structural parameters of the established order, and even *idealized* in the name of *"real politics."*

One of the most acute aspects of this problem in the midst of the present global crisis, requiring *urgent solution* in the interest of gaining control over the perilous determinations of capital's *uncontrollability,* concerns the question of *responsibility.* By its innermost nature capital's socioeconomic order is a system of *institutionalized irresponsibility* on the *overall societal plane.* As a system of competing special interests, it is capable of assigning responsibility only to limited partial domains but not to society as a whole, which must be divided and managed, in an adversarial fashion, on the material, political, and cultural ground of capital's insuperable *antagonistic second order mediations.* True to form, heads of governments declared recently that *none* of them could be held responsible for what happened and continues to happen today, because the crisis is *global.* And that absolves *all* of the leading decision-makers of capital—with the exception of the derisively few criminals like Madoff who are caught in the act—of their grave responsibility in imposing immense suffering on the great masses of the people.

However, it is quite impossible to envisage a viable solution to our global crisis without assuming *full responsibility* for the ongoing developments, especially in a *globally interconnected* and necessarily *interacting* system. But of course the personifications of capital, following the imperatives of their system's perverse logic, could

never do that in the interest of society as a whole. Only the hegemonic alternative of labor as a comprehensively planned and, thereby, historically sustainable mode of societal reproduction is capable
of responding to that urgent need under the conditions of our aggravating systemic crisis.

At the same time, it must be also stressed that *responsibility* without *real powers of decision-making* can only be an *imposition from
above* and is, therefore, unworkable even in the short run and more
so on a historical scale. The implosion of the societies of "actually
existing socialism"—due to a large extent to the *recalcitrance* of its
labor force, politically controlled from above—offers tragically con-
clusive evidence for that. Nor is it possible to believe that a great
intensification of authoritarian capitalist control measures, no doubt
increasingly advocated in some quarters today, could solve this
problem on a durable basis. The devastating failures of the past—
from Mussolini's fascism and Hitler's Nazi-Fascism to the various
U.S.-sponsored dictatorships in Latin America, including Brazil
and Pinochet's Chile—clearly refute the viability of such projects.

The *defensive articulation* of the labor movement in the twentieth century resulted in great setbacks also in this respect. The
much-needed *solidarity* among the members of the working class
for assuming the historical *responsibility*, inseparable from their
hegemonic alternative to the ruling order, is undermined by the necessary *divisiveness* of action confined primarily to the improvement
of *sectional interests*. Capital could, thus, successfully play some sections of its class adversary against the others, *greatly weakening* the
overall emancipatory power of the working class as a whole in which
full class solidarity remained a distant prospect on the horizon.
However, without *class solidarity* and the closely associated vision
of a comprehensive *strategic alternative* to the existing order, there
can be no question of fulfilling the responsibility required for overcoming the acute structural crisis of the system.

Accordingly, the necessity to consign *defensiveness, divisiveness,
and the primary pursuit of sectional interests* to the past is the
absolutely vital condition for becoming able to assume this urgently
required *responsibility*, without which *none* of the fundamental

issues of the unfolding global structural crisis can be solved, in fulfillment of labor's strategically viable comprehensive historical alternative. And, naturally, that is inconceivable without passionately adopted and fully shared *class solidarity* as the proper mode of operation of labor's qualitatively different social metabolic reproduction. *Real powers of decision-making, shared on a substantively equitable basis among all working members of society, in the spirit of class solidarity and freely assumed responsibility:* these are the defining characteristics of labor's hegemonic alternative, in sharp contrast to the incurably destructive logic of the capital system of our time.

In this sense, both the unions and the parties of the working class must be *combatively industrial and political* at the same time. Their emancipatory success is feasible only if their *fundamental orienting principle* is an *all-embracing change in the framework of societal reproduction.* For *immediate* demands and concerns, even limited ones, can only be realized on a lasting basis within the envisaged comprehensive strategic framework of labor's hegemonic alternative. That is also the necessary condition for solving our present crisis of truly all-embracing proportions. Defensive wage-negotiating and political tinkering in the failed tradition of reformist accommodation can only aggravate our global crisis.

7. LABOR'S HISTORICAL ALTERNATIVE TO CAPITAL'S SOCIAL ORDER

DS: What should be the action of the political instruments of the working class in its movements? And what should be their relationship with the State's institutions, like governments and parliaments? How could the unions and the workers parties help to improve anticapitalist awareness and how could they help to foster a rebirth of socialist consciousness, especially in the imperialist countries?

IM: We have to recall in this context Herbert Marcuse, whom I consider our real comrade, despite differences. For he identified some major challenges we have to face, even if the explanations offered by him were questionable. Two of his deeply felt concerns, formulated in the postwar period of rather undisturbed capital-expansion, are directly relevant here. They are inseparable from one another. The first was his conviction that capitalism succeeded in solving its crises of the past, and now we are confronted by the more bewildering power of *organized capitalism*, in place of *crisis capitalism*. The second is a close companion to the first, explaining in a significant way for him even the success of organized capitalism. It stated that the *working class itelf* had become *integrated* into the post-crisis capitalist system, making it, therefore, necessary to think of some alternative historic subject—like his "outsiders" and the student movement—as the required actor of change.

Sadly, after the great disappointment which he suffered in his expectation of an emancipatory outsider, Marcuse adopted, toward the end of his life, a totally pessimistic perspective, which is conceptualized in his book *The Aesthetic Dimension*.

As we know from our historical experience, the success of organized capitalism was *conjunctural*. It extended over the postwar period of reconstruction and capital-expansion only, and its "welfare capitalist" achievements applied to a very limited number of Western capitalist countries. Accordingly, crisis had to return sooner or later and with a vengeance, in view of the capital system's irreconcilable global antagonisms.

However, the other challenge identified by Marcuse presented a much more difficult problem. The signs and paralyzing setbacks of working-class integration seemed to be predominant in every capitalistically advanced country, spreading also in the so-called Third World with the process of industrial expansion dominated by transnational capital. The suffocating tentacles of international finance capital—also dominated by the major capitalist countries, above all the United States, with its privileged role in running the IMF, the World Bank, and the global trade organizations—added a major dimension to this regressively integrative process.

Yet, the question to be decided was: is *labor itself*, the only viable *hegemonic alternative* to capital's social order, really integrated into the system? For if the answer was an emphatic "yes," as

Marcuse thought, the pessimistic perspective was inescapable, carrying despair with it for all of those who once believed in the realization of the advocated historical alternative. That is the context in which the role of the governments and trade unions of the working class requires critical examination, together with the political framework of parliament. For the latter remains ruthlessly dominated by *capital's extra-parliamentary force* pretending to be a genuine parliamentary interlocutor, consigning the reformist parties and occasional governments of the working class to utter powerlessness through the enforcement of the rules of the parliamentary game. The self-defeating division of the political arm from the industrial arm prescribed by the parliamentary rules of the game was the most effective institutional embodiment of this process of real disarmament.

Having lost its material power for instituting systemic change through industrial and structurally significant political transformative action, the reformist *political as well as trade union leadership* of the working class had to become *undoubtedly integrated* into the system, divorcing itself from the working class in the name of promoting the interests of modern business and industry. And, revealingly, this *self-disarming integration of leadership* was not confined to the reformist parties. The logic of the same operational setting, under the extra-parliamentary rule of capital, in due course dragged along with it also the biggest Communist Parties of Western Europe, the Italian and the French.

The working class itself, as the controlling subject of the hegemonic alternative to capital's rule cannot be integrated into the system. For in order to be able to do that, the *structural antagonisms* would have to be permanently eliminated from capital's societal reproductive order. To be sure, the working class can be temporarily deprived of its class-conscious leadership; it can be silenced and even paralyzed for a shorter or longer historical period. But it cannot accept capital's destructive—and ultimately self-destructive—mode of antagonistic societal reproduction as its natural and permanent condition of existence. This is why the radical rearticulation of the socialist movement, in opposition to its integrated leadership, is an unavoidable challenge of our time. It is inconceivable even to properly evaluate the critical issues of our present global crisis without that, not to mention solve them on a lasting basis.

This means that much has to be started anew, on the basis of genuine *mass* involvement and in the spirit of Marx's original call for the development of *"communist mass consciousness."* The *destructive extra-parliamentary force of capital* cannot be defeated through respectful conformity to the rules of the parliamentary game. It requires the extra-parliamentary mobilization of combative mass action in support of the radical political forces of the working class active in parliament.

All that implies also a major change in the orientation of the industrial arm of the working class. Brazil has succeeded in developing a most important radical movement, with deep roots in the popular masses, the MST or Landless Workers Movement. It is a movement carrying out its own initiatives and refusing to be integrated into the ruling order. The further expansion and strengthening of such mass-based and strategically-conscious movements is a great hope for our future. Similarly, one of the greatest challenges ahead of us is the organizationally secured mobilization of the countless millions of the *unemployed*, whose number is bound to get much greater in the future. The traditional sectorial orientation of the industrial arm could not even notice their existence, let alone pay the required—remedially effective—attention to their devastating plight.

This cannot be left the way it is at the present. Not only because it is morally reprehensible to do so, but also because the radical mobilization of the unemployed millions—and in global terms *billions*—potentially offers a major additional strength to the socialist movement. *Solidarity* is both a vital socialist value and a major source of emancipatory power. Labor's hegemonic alternative cannot prevail against capital without full solidarity in its own ranks. The workers in the dominant capitalist countries may take longer to learn these historical lessons than their brothers and sisters in the rest of the world. But learn they must and will under the inescapable

impact of the deepening structural crisis. There are hopeful signs
pointing in that direction, as mentioned earlier, even in the most
privileged countries.

8. A RADICAL POLITICAL MOVEMENT
IS UNTHINKABLE WITHOUT THE CREATIVE
SELF-EDUCATION OF ITS MEMBERS

DS: For us, an important element in the Brazilian evaluation of the Left
in the twentieth century is the tragic contempt for a deep Marxist
education. What is, in your vision, the place of Marxist studies in a
workers party? What alternative weapons could we use in the ideological struggle for workers consciousness?

IM: The neglect of Marxist education is unfortunately prevalent also in
the capitalistically advanced countries. This is not only due to the
institutionalized power of the ruling ideology, dominating the mass
media almost completely, but also to the reformist political tradition
that accommodated itself to the ruling order. The only political education relevant to the reformist parties today is the electoral prepara-
tory process of canvassing at doorsteps, the operation of the so-
called focus groups of ludicrously narrow-minded opinion research, and the spinning of information and false information, for the
purpose of systematically (and often cynically) misleading the population while retaining electoral support for the parliamentary
governments. The primary function of such governments is now
confined to constituting the electorally saleable public relations
façade of capital's destructive imperatives.

When we remind ourselves of the history of the socialist movement, the contrast is striking. For in its early stages the role
assigned to political education was in fact most important. To take
only one example, Rosa Luxemburg was not only a great revolutionary leader of the working class but also a most devoted teacher
in the Party's educational organs, writing some of her most important works—in Marxist economics and political theory—for the
purpose of developing militant socialist consciousness. Similar
activities characterized the life of most social democratic—and of

course communist—parties for several decades from the time of their foundation.

The unholy consensus around the mindless slogan that "there is no alternative" and the associated degradation of political activity to the level of creating a broad electoral alliance had successfully put an end to all of that, destroying in the end even the major Western Communist Parties. This is how it came about that Bettino Craxi, the leader of the once radical Socialist Party, Pietro Nenni's Party, had to flee his country and end his life in Tunisia, so as to avoid a jail term for corruption. Meanwhile his master, Silvio Berlusconi, was elected not once but three times to the position of Prime Minister in Italy. This is in Italy, the same country in which the Party of Antonio Gramsci once represented a combative political force in the interest of radical change.

Obviously, none of the vital emancipatory tasks can be realized without a fundamental change in this respect. No party can call itself radical without engaging, with sustained determination, in the work of radical political education. Without the pursuit of a *comprehensive strategic design* that can enable us to address both *immediate demands* and more distant transformative objectives, we are bound to remain at the mercy of the global crisis. But how could such a comprehensive strategic design be pursued without the political and theoretical awareness required for elaborating and understanding the tasks ahead by the great masses of the people?

Such education is not some kind of academic exercise or an equally sterile sectarian political exercise, whereby individuals must learn what is in books laid out by experts and authorities. Some notorious authoritarian party seminars in "actually existing socialism" operated on that basis, with *counterproductive* effects. Political education can be successful only if it truly involves the people in the *ongoing development of socialist consciousness* appropriate to the necessarily changing tasks and challenges. The best form of education is *self-education*, within a combatively dedicated comradely and cooperative framework. People really appropriate in a positive way what is made available to them and transform it into their own when they are directly involved, as an integral part, in a meaningful interactive process.

A radical socialist political party, committed to the realization of both the immediate demands and the long-term comprehensive and emancipatory transformation, is a most suitable framework for this kind of creative self-education. For it is engaged in offering to its members, and through their intermediary to society as a whole, both the tangible tasks to be actively embraced by them, shared on a substantively equitable basis by all members of the party, and at the same time some of the most important strategic instruments for the accomplishment of the adopted tasks. This is the only way in which the much-needed political education of our time can significantly contribute to the solution of the present crisis, within a socialist overall perspective.

The way the expression "mass party" is used is frequently most inaccurate. It means in reality not only the total absence of the active involvement of people in solving their problems but also the lack of organizational belonging to the party in question. The actual membership of the purported mass party of New Labour in Britain is quite negligible. Nor could one speak of political education associated with this kind of party in any meaningful sense of the term. The only sense in which such parties are mass parties is in their dubious function of supplying *mass electoral fodder*. And even that is at times accomplished only at a scandalously low rate due to general disillusionment with institutionalized politics. This highly embarrassing fact indicates an astronomical distance from the political education and awareness that once characterized even the reformist social democratic and labor parties.

Thus, the need for a proper political education, actively involving the great masses of the people, is greater today in the midst of our global structural crisis than ever before. But, as things stand today, to turn the need for real political education into reality is unthinkable without the development of an organizationally coherent radical movement of genuine mass allegiance. This relationship asserts itself the other way round, as well. For it is unthinkable to establish a radical political movement of genuine mass allegiance without the passionately undertaken and instituted work of vital political education. And that is feasible only by successfully uniting the industrial arm of labor with its political arm in the spirit of an all-embracing emancipatory project. This demands the radicalization of the still primarily reformist trade union movement.

Notes

FOREWORD

1. Chávez first called Mészáros "Pathfinder" (Señalador de caminos)—referring to his role in illuminating the transition to socialism—in an inscription that he wrote in a copy of Simon Rodriguez's *Collected Works*, which he gave to Mészáros at a dinner in the Miraflores Palace on Septermber 10, 2001. On the same occasion they discussed Mészáros's *Beyond Capital*, with Chávez exhibiting the copious notes he had made in his copy.
2. Hugo Chávez, *AloPresidente*, May 3, 2009.
3. On the economic crisis itself see John Bellamy Foster and Fred Magdoff, *The Great Financial Crisis: Causes and Consequences* (New York: Monthly Review Press, 2009); also pp. 181–85 of this book.
4   The fact that Mészáros understood this from the start as "the structural crisis of capital," and not merely a conjunctural economic crisis, can be seen by looking at Chapter 3 of this book, "The Necessity of Social Control," originally delivered as a lecture in January 1971, on his receipt of the Issac Deutscher Prize for his *Marx's Theory of Alienation*.
5. In addition to the present book see István Mészáros, "The Communal System and the Principle of Self-Critique," *Monthly Review* 59, no. 10 (March 2008), 33–56.
6. Jacob Burckhardt, *Reflections on History* (Indianapolis: Liberty Press, 1979), 213, 224.

INTRODUCTION: THE SUBSTANCE OF THE CRISIS

1. The origin of this book was my correspondence with István Mészáros in January, 2009, when I sent him an article I had just published on the current

crisis. I was then trying to briefly underline the strength, density, and originali-
ty of his critical analysis, in contrast to the total ignorance of the widest seg-
ments of capital—intellectuals, managers, governments—after decades of
depressing apologetics preaching the *eternity of capital,* failing to realize that it
was on the brink of melting and liquefaction. Hence the idea of compiling a
short collection of some of his articles and interviews, stretching back to the
earliest works so as to highlight his analysis and demonstrate a continuity
essential to the understanding of the most basic and decisive elements of a crisis that left the ideologues of the system astonished and orphaned, and all those
others who had accepted the End of History thesis, what Mészáros ironically
called "pseudo-Hegelian Fukuyamization."

2.   It is essential to underline that, for Mészáros, *capital* and *capitalism* are *distinct*
phenomena. The system of capital, he wrote, came before capitalism and was
present in post-capitalist societies as well. Capitalism is *one* possible form of
capital, one of its *historical variants*, present in the phase characterized by the
real subsumption of labor under capital, what Marx called mature capitalism.
Just as there was *capital* before the expansion of capitalism (such as merchant
or usury capital), the recent forms of socio-metabolic metabolism allow us to
see the persistence of capital even *after* capitalism, through the constitution of
what Mészáros called "the post-capitalist capital system," exemplified by the
USSR and countries of Eastern Europe. Those *post-capitalist* countries did not
manage to break away from the system of social metabolism of capital, and the
conceptual identification between capital and capitalism made, according to
the author, *every* revolutionary experience in the century unable to overcome
the *system of social metabolism of capital* (the complex characterized by a hierarchical division of labor, whose vital needs are subordinated to capital). On the
Soviet experience, see in particular Chapter XVII, items 2/3/4 of *Beyond
Capital: Toward a Theory of Transition*. On the most important differences
between capitalism and the Soviet system, see in particular the summary on
pages 630–631.

3.   The core of the *system of social metabolism* of capital is constituted by the tri-
pod of capital, wage labor, and the state, three fundamental, closely interrelated
dimensions, making the supersession of capital impossible without overcoming
the components of the system. According to Mészáros, it is therefore not
enough to do away with one or even two of the pillars of the system of social
metabolism of capital, but it is imperative to transcend all three. This thesis has
an explanatory power that stands in stark contrast to all that has been written
so far about the fall of the Soviet Union and of the countries wrongly defined as
the "socialist bloc."

4.   During a British workers' demonstration in February, 2009 there was a sign
reading "Put British Workers First." The demonstration was against the hiring

of Portuguese and Italian immigrant labor for below-average salaries. As old and fair as the struggle for wage equality is, the exclusion of foreign workers is clearly xenophobic. Such demonstrations are becoming more common in Europe, Japan, the United States, and many other corners of the world.

5. *Global Wage Report 2008*, International Labour Organization, November 2008.

6. *Employment Overview for Latin America and the Caribbean, International Labour Organization,* January 2009.

7. First published in the Brazilian periodical *Escrita Ensaio*, Anno V, no. 11–12 (Summer 1983), 105–124. A shorter version of this article was delivered as a lecture in Athens in April 1983. The article is reprinted in full in Part IV of *Beyond Capital* (Monthly Review Press, 2000): 937–951.

8. "Notes from the Editors," *Monthly Review*, Vol. 60, No. 10 (March 2009), 64.

CHAPTER ONE: THE UNFOLDING CRISIS
AND THE RELEVANCE OF MARX

1. This chapter presents a lecture written for a meeting held at Conway Hall in London on October 21, 2008.

2. All of these quotations are taken from an editorial in *The Economist*, October 11, 2008, 13.

3. Special section, *The Economist*, October 11, 2008, 3.

4. Ibid.

5. Ibid., 4.

6. Ibid.

7. Ibid., 6.

8. Shii Kazuo in *Japan Press Weekly,* October 2008, 20.

9. Andrew Lorenz and Jeff Randall, "Ford prepares for global revolution," *The Sunday Times,* March 27 1994, sec. 3. Quoted in my book, *Beyond Capital* (London: Merlin Press, 1995), 165.

10. "A bail-out that passed. In the slipstream of Wall Street's woes, the Big Three land a huge subsidy," *The Economist*, October 4, 2008, 82.

11. Ibid., 83.

12. Lehman Brothers, one of the principal private merchant banks, had a gearing ratio of 30 to 1. That is bad enough!

13. "Fannie Mae and Freddie Mac: End of Illusions," *The Economist,* July 19–25, 2008, 84.

14. "A Brief Family History: Toxic Fudge," *The Economist,* July 19–25, 2008, 84.

15. "Fannie Mae and Freddie Mac: End of illusions," *The Economist,* July 19–25, 2008, 85.

16.   *Beyond Capital*, 962–963. The section from which this quote is taken is repro-
      duced in its entirety in Chapter 2, "The Present Crisis," in this book.
17.   See "Qualitative Growth in Utilization: The Only Viable Economy," section
      9.5 of my *The Challenge and Burden of Historical Time* (New York: Monthly
      Review Press, 2008), 272–93.
18.   Mervyn King's endorsement, on the back cover of Martin Wolf's book, *Why
      Globalization Works* (New Haven: Yale University Press, 2004).
19.   In "Education—Beyond Capital," Opening Lecture delivered at the *Fórum
      Mundial de Educação*, Porto Allegre, July 28, 2004. Published in Spanish in *La
      educación más allá del capital* (Buenos Aires: Siglo Veintiuno Editores/Clacso
      Coediciones, 2008). See also the chapter "Why Capitalist Globalization
      Cannot Work?" in my *The Challenge and Burden of Historical Time*, 380–398;
      Spanish edition: *El desafío y la carga del tiempo histórico* (Caracas: Vadell
      Hermanos Editores/Clacso Coediciónes, 2008), 371–389.

CHAPTER TWO: THE PRESENT CRISIS

1.   Written in August 1987 and first published in the Brazilian periodical *Ensaio*,
      No. 17–18, Numero Especial, 159–71. Republished in István Mészáros,
      Beyond Capital (London: Merlin Press, 1995), 952–964.
2.   *Computer Weekly,* December 19, 1985.
3.   Michael Heseltine's resignation statement, January 9, 1986.
4.   *Computer Weekly,* June 13, 1985.
5.   Quoted in Mary Kaldor, "Towards a High-Tech Europe?," *New Socialist*, No.
      35, February 1986, 10.
6.   See the discussion of state intervention in the service of capital-expansion in
      Chapter 3, "The Necessity of Social Control," in this book.
7.   Kaldor, "Towards a High-Tech Europe?" The author gives some revealing
      examples in her article: "Electrical industries are interesting to look at because
      this sector has both military and commercial markets. You can, for example,
      compare the share of government-funded R&D (predominantly defence-relat-
      ed, except in West Germany) in the electrical industries as a whole, and com-
      petitiveness in office machinery and computers, electronic components, and
      electrical machinery. Apart from office machinery and computers, where the
      large military market makes the U.S. competitive, the inverse relation between
      defence R&D and competitiveness is quite marked. Another interesting exam-
      ple is chemicals. The only high technology sector in which the U.K. is very
      competitive, as defined by the OECD, is drugs and medicine. This is one area
      where military R&D—and its influence—is negligible. Concern about declin-
      ing competitiveness in manufacturing has prompted a series of official reports

in both Britain and the United States. In Britain, two reports—one by the House of Lords Select Committee on Science and Technology, the other by Sir Ieuan Maddocks, on behalf of the National Economic Development Council—argued that the high level of defence R&D is a major reason for the failure of Britain to exploit science and technology effectively enough to increase the competitiveness of British manufacturing." See Kaldor, 11.

8.   Quoted in Ibid.

9.   *Computer Weekly*, July 18, 1985.

10. Ibid., February 19, 1987.

11. See the editorial article in *Computer Weekly*, entitled "Blame Reagan, not U.S. Trade." The congenital illusions of the liberal position are well illustrated by the editorial's title itself. As if the actions of the U.S. administration could be separated from, and opposed to, the interests of U.S. trade.

12. Ibid., January 16, 1986.

13. Ibid., June 13, 1985.

14. *Parliamentary debates*, February 4, 1986.

15. "Selling off, and shrugging yet again," *The Guardian*, February 5, 1986.

16. Ibid.

17. As reported in *The Guardian*, February 5, 1986.

18. See Samir Amin, Giovanni Arrighi, André Gunder Frank, and Immanuel Wallerstein, *Dynamics of Global Crisis* (London: Macmillan, 1982).

19. Paul Baran, *The Political Economy of Growth* (Monthly Review Press: New York, 1957), vii.

20. Ibid. Baran quotes on the same page also another passage from the bitterly realist words of the London *Economist* (November 17, 1957): "We must learn that we are not the Americans' equals now, and cannot be. We have a right to state our minimum national interests and expect the Americans to respect them. But this done, we must look for their lead."

21. "U.S. trade deficit hits quarterly record," *Financial Times*, August 27, 1987.

22. Andrew Lorenz and Frank Kane, "Barings seeks rescue buyer," *The Sunday Times*, February 26, 1995.

23. Ibid.

24. Ibid.

25. "Where a slump might start," *The Economist*, June 17, 1995.

26. Walden Bello, Shea Cunningham, and Bill Rau, *Dark Victory: The United States, Structural Adjustment, and Global Poverty* (Oakland: Institute for Food and Development Policy, 1994).

27. Martin Hart-Landsberg, "Dark Victory: Capitalism Unchecked," *Monthly Review* 46, no. 10 (March 1995), 55.

28. "The G7 at an impasse," *Financial Times*, April 28, 1992.

CHAPTER THREE: THE NECESSITY OF SOCIAL CONTROL

1. *Marx's Theory of Alienation* by István Mészáros was awarded the Isaac
    Deutscher Memorial Prize in 1970. The first Isaac Deutscher Memorial lec-
    ture, on "The Necessity of Social Control" was delivered at the London School
    of Economics and Political Science on January 26, 1971. Published as a sepa-
    rate volume, under the same title, by Merlin Press, London, 1971.

2. Isaac Deutscher, *The Unfinished Revolution* (Oxford: Oxford University Press,
    1967), 110-4.

3. W.W. Rostow, *The Stages of Economic Growth: A Non-Communist Manifesto*
    (Cambridge: Cambridge University Press, 1960), 157-164.

4. People often forget that President Kennedy was directly responsible for the
    escalating U.S. involvement in Vietnam, inaugurating a whole series of disas-
    trous policies conceived on the basis of "theories" like the one quoted above.

5. Here is a graphic example of tautological apologetics based on a retrospective
    reconstruction of the past in the key of an idealized present of U.S. capital-
    ism: "The relative inter-war stagnation in Western Europe was due not to
    long-run diminishing return but to the *failure* of Western Europe to create a
    setting in which its national societies moved promptly into the age of high
    mass consumption, yielding new leading sectors. And this *failure,* in turn,
    was due mainly to a *failure* to create initial full employment in the post-1920
    setting of the terms of trade. Similarly the protracted depression of the
    United States in the 1930s was due not to long-run diminishing returns, but
    to a *failure* to create an initial renewed setting of full employment, through
    public policy, which *would have permitted* the new leading sectors of subur-
    ban housing, the diffusion of automobiles, durable consumers' goods and
    services to roll forward beyond 1929." See Rostow, *The Stages of Economic
    Growth,* 155.

    Thus, "failures" (crises and recessions) are explained by the failure to real-
    ize the conditions which would have permitted the avoidance of those unfortu-
    nate failures, by producing the present-day pattern of capitalist high-consump-
    tion which is, of course, the *non plus ultra* of everything. How those unfortu-
    nate, failure-explanatory failures came into being, we are not told. Since, how-
    ever, the point of the whole exercise is the propagation of Rostow's objective
    and non-parochial *Non-Communist Manifesto* as the ultimate salvation of U.S.
    dominated world capitalism, by implication we can take it that the failures in
    question must have been due to the absence of this retrospective-tautological
    economic and political wisdom. By what failures he would explain today's ris-
    ing unemployment and the associated symptoms of serious structural distur-
    bances in the United States as well as in other parts of the capitalist world of
    "high mass-consumption," "suburban housing," etc. must remain, unfortunate-

ly, a mystery to us, since there are no "new leading sectors" in sight whose creation "would have permitted" the avoidance of present-day failures.

6. Rostow, 163.

7. Karl Marx and Friedrich Engels, *The German Ideology*, 55–6.

8. Ibid., 56.

9. I have discussed several related problems in "Contingent and Necessary Class Consciousness," my contribution to *Aspects of History and Class Consciousness*, edited by István Mészáros (London: Routledge & Kegan Paul, 1971); reprinted in István Mészáros, *Philosophy, Ideology and Social Science* (Brighton: Harvester Press, 1986), 57–104.

10. See Karl Marx, *Grundrisse der Kritik der politischen Ökonomie* (Berlin, 1953), 593–594.

11. This is how the *Voice of America* introduces its program of interviews with intellectuals on "Man and his Survival": "The order of importance of great tasks has changed. Today no longer the clash of *national interests*, or the struggle for *political power* occupy the first place; nor indeed the elimination of *social injustice*. The outstanding issue by now is whether or not mankind will succeed in securing the conditions of its survival in a world it has transformed. . . . No wonder that the President of the United States has dedicated two thirds of his latest 'State of the Union' message to the question of how to rehabilitate the environment from pollution. What happens, though, if man, instead of thinking about his own survival, *wastes his energies in fighting for the relative truth of various ideologies and social-political systems?* What are the first steps mankind ought to take in order *to reform itself and the world?*" Further comment is quite unnecessary, thanks to the transparency of these lines.

12. A capability so far very effectively paralyzed by the guardians of the ruling order. For a penetrating analysis of the dynamic potentialities of the "mass media" see Hans Magnus Enzensberger, "Constituents of a Theory of the Media," *New Left Review*, No. 64 (November–December 1970), 13–36.

13. E.J. Mishan, *The Cost of Economic Growth*, (Harmondsworth: Penguin Books, 1969), 225.

14. November 6, 1957.

15. On Saturday, March 17, 1883, the London *Times* published the following notice: "Our Paris correspondent informs us of the death of Dr. Karl Marx, which occurred last Wednesday, in London. He was born at Cologne, in the year 1818. At the age of 25 he had to leave his native country and take refuge in France, on account of the Radical opinions expressed in a paper of which he was editor. In France he gave himself up to the study of philosophy and politics, and made himself so obnoxious to the Prussian Government by his writings that he was expelled from France, and lived for a time in Belgium. In 1847

he assisted at the Working Men's Congress in London, and was one of the authors of the 'Manifesto of the Communist Party.' After the Revolution of 1848 he returned to Paris, and afterwards to his native city of Cologne, from which he was again expelled for his revolutionary writings, and after escaping from imprisonment in France, he settled in London. From this time he was one of the leaders of the Socialist Party in Europe, and in 1866 he became its acknowledged chief. He wrote pamphlets on various subjects, but his chief work was 'Le Capital,' an attack on the whole capitalist system. For some time he had been suffering from weak health."

What is remarkable about this piece is not only its provenance from Paris but also the way in which the class solidarity of international capital is revealed in it through reporting the concerted reactions of governments (the Prussian Government is annoyed—thus—the French Government acts) to the "obnoxiousness" of the man who dared to write "an attack on the whole capitalist system."

16. Editorial, *The Times,* October 17, 1970.

17. *Ibid.,* October, 20 1970.

18. Marx's comments on the Prussian censorship instructions throw an interesting light on this "liberal" mode of arguing: "'Nothing will be tolerated which opposes Christian religion in general or a particular doctrine in a frivolous and hostile manner.' How cleverly put: *frivolous, hostile.* The adjective 'frivolous' appeals to the *citizen's sense of propriety* and is the exoteric term in the *public view;* but the adjective 'hostile' is whispered into the *censor's ear* and becomes the *legal interpretation* of frivolity." In our quotation the corresponding terms are: "the influence of society" (for the citizen's sense of propriety) and "all the power of government" (for the authoritarian state official's ear).

19. As the editors of the *Trade Union Register* rightly emphasize: "The similarities between the two documents [i.e., the Tory *Fair Deal at Work* and Labour's *In Place of Strife*] are considerable, and certainly more substantial than their differences. This consensus reflects the whole tendency in orthodox political circles to assume that workers (not necessarily trade unions) have too much freedom and power in the exercise of strike action and other forms of industrial collective pressure, and that it is legitimate for the state to legislate with a view to restraining and limiting those freedoms and powers. In view of the enormous recent increases in the authority and influence of the state itself, and of large irresponsible private industrial and commercial companies, against which the independent forces of organized labour alone stand as a guarantee of ultimate civic and political liberties, the consensus view prevailing in the political parties of the centre and right requires the most vigorous and thorough opposition from the

labour movement." See Ken Coates, Tony Topham, and Michael Barratt Brown, eds., *Trade Union Register 1970* (London: Merlin Press, 1970), 276.

20.   Barbara Castle, "The Bad Bosses' Charter," *New Statesman,* October 16, 1970.

21.   When Mr. Heath nationalizes Rolls Royce (after his repeated denunciation of the measure of nationalization as "doctrinaire socialist nonsense"), all he carries out is, of course, the "nationalization" of capitalist bankruptcy in a key sector of commodity production. The fact, though, that the immediate cause of this step was a contract negotiated by the outgoing Labour Government (envisaging the balancing of enormous private losses from public funds) only highlights the surrender of both parties to the dictates of the prevailing capitalist structure of production. Such dictates prescribe the transference of the non-profitable branches of industry into the "public" (i.e., state-bureaucracy controlled) sector so that they can be turned into further subsidies at the service of monopoly capital. Thankfully, this particular act of "nationalization" has been carried out by a Conservative Government—which makes it a less mystifying event. For had it been implemented by a Labour Government, it would have been loudly hailed as a great landmark of "pragmatic socialism."

22.   Karl Marx, *The Poverty of Philosophy* (London: Lawrence & Wishart, n.d.), 123.

23.   They are in the process of disintegration precisely because—due to their inherent contradictions—they are unable to cope with the vital functions they are supposed to carry out in the totality of social intercourse.

CHAPTER FOUR: RADICAL POLITICS AND TRANSITION TO SOCIALISM: REFLECTIONS ON MARX'S CENTENARY

1.   First published in the Brazilian periodical *Escrita Ensaio,* Año V, No. 11–12, 1983, 105–124. Republished in István Mészáros, *Beyond Capital* (London: Merlin Press, 1995), 937–951.

2.   Karl Marx, "Marginal Notes on Adolf Wagner" in *Value Studies by Marx* (London: New Park Publications, 1976), 228.

3.   V. I. Lenin, *Collected Works,* vol. 31, (Moscow: Progress Publishers, 1965), 56. Lenin's emphases.

4.   Marx insisted that human beings must change "from top to bottom the conditions of their industrial and political existence, and consequently their whole manner of being." See Karl Marx, *The Poverty of Philosophy* (London: Lawrence & Wishart, London, n.d.), 123.

CHAPTER FIVE: BOLÍVAR AND CHÁVEZ
THE SPIRIT OF RADICAL DETERMINATION

1.   Published in *Margem esquerda,* November 2006, 76–108; and in *Monthly Review* 59, No. 3 (July–August 2007): 55–84.

2.   Bolívar quoted in John Lynch, *Simón Bolívar: A Life* (New Haven: Yale University Press, 2006), 26. Note: the translations from Bolívar in this chapter are by the author and differ slightly from previously published English translations cited in this chapter.

3.   Simón Bolívar, *Selected Works,* (New York: Colonial Press, 1951) 2:603.

4.   Bolívar, *Selected Works,* 1:195.

5.   Bolívar, *Selected Works,* 2:732; Lynch, *Simón Bolívar,* 264.

6.   President Clinton's Labor Secretary, Robert B. Reich—a former Harvard University Professor—advocated the forceful adoption of *"positive economic nationalism"* by his own country. See his book, *The Work of Nations: A Blueprint for the Future* (Hemel Hempstead: Simon & Schuster, 1994), 311.

7.   Moynihan proclaimed, in an authoritarian way, that democracy is not "a universal option for all nations" in his *Pandaemonium: Ethnicity in International Relations,* (Oxford: Oxford University Press, 1993), 169.

8.   Bolívar, *Selected Works,* 2:737.

9.   Referred to in the speech made by President Chávez, "La Revolución Bolivariana y la construcción del socialism en el siglo XXI," XVI Festival Mundial de la Juventud y los Estudiantes, Caracas, August 13, 2005.

10. Bolívar quoted in Lynch, *Simón Bolívar,* 126.

11. See José Martí, "Discurso," pronounced in Hardman Hall, New York, October 10, 1890; and "La Verdad Sobre los Estados Unidos," *Patria,* April 17, 1884.

12. Bolívar, *Selected Works,* 1:119.

13. See in particular "Hay que ir organizando un gran movimiento continental," a speech delivered at the Universidad Nacional de Asunción, República de Paraguay, June 20, 2005; and "La Revolución Bolivariana y la construcción del socialismo en el siglo XXI," delivered in Caracas, August 13, 2005. For an important recent interview see Manuel Cabieses, "?Qué diferenciaría al socialismo del siglo XXI de aquel socialismo que se derrumbo? / ?Donde va Chávez?," *Punto Final,* No. 598, August 19, 2005.

14. On December 6, 1998 Hugo Chávez Frias was elected President of Venezuela in the first round of the elections, with a resounding 56.24 percent of the vote. Thus, all the other candidates put together had to content themselves with no more than 43.76 percent of the vote cast.

     The following material was first published in István Mészáros, *Beyond Capital* (London: Merlin Press, 1995), 709–712.

15. Jean-Jacques Rousseau, *The Social Contract* (New York: Everyman's Library, 1993), 78.

16. Ibid., 79.

17. Ibid., 42.

18. Hugo Chávez Frias, *Pueblo, Sufragio y Democracia* (Yara: Ediciones MBR-200, 1993), 5-6.

19. Ibid., 9.

20. Ibid., 11.

21. Ibid., 8-11.

22. Ibid., 9.

23. Rather the opposite, in that always new military targets for the allegedly crisis-solving pursuit of unashamedly aggressive *"preemptive wars"*—to be waged against countries ranging from Iran and Syria to North Korea and other arbitrarily designated members of the so-called Axis of Evil—are repeatedly advocated by the most reactionary political leaders of the global hegemonic imperialist power and urged on by their even more extremist backroom boys. Thereby, wishfully but quite absurdly projecting as the necessary beneficial solution the dictatorial imposition of a mode of action which could only aggravate the system's problems to the point of a catastrophic global explosion.

24. "seria nefasto, así lo creo, que permitamos que el Foro Social Mundial se folklorice, que se convierta en un encuentro folklórico de todos los años. Encuentro turístico, folklórico, eso seria terrible, porque estaríamos sencillamente perdiendo el tiempo y no estamos para perder el tiempo. . . . Creo que a nosotros no nos está dado el pensar en los siglos futuros . . . no estamos para perder tiempo, se trata de salvar la vida en el planeta, se trata de salvar la especie humana, cambiando el rumbo de la historia, cambiando el mundo." See Hugo Chávez, "Closing Speech at the Sixth World Social Forum," January 27, 2006.

25. For instance, when a radical political leader is brought to the position of heading the government of his or her country by an electoral process—to be followed by the establishment of a Constitutional Assembly—and not by an all-embracing social and political revolution. It is enough to think in this respect of the contrast between Venezuela and Cuba.

26. Bolívar, *Selected Works*, 1:192.

27. For instance, when addressing an assembly of soldiers in this way: "¡Soldados! Vosotros lo sabeis. *La igualdad, la libertad y la independencia* son nuestra divisa. ¿La humanidad no ha recobrado sus derechos por nuestras leyes? Nuestras armas, ¿no han roto las *cadenas de los esclavos? La odiosa diferencia de clases y colores*, ¿no ha sido abolida para siempre? Los bienes nacionales, ¿no se han mandado repartir entre vosotros? ¿La fortuna, el saber y la glória no os esperan? ¿Vuestros méritos no son recompensados con profusión, or *por lo menos por justicia?*" See Felipe Larrazabal, *Vita y escritos del*

Libertador, vol. 2, (Caracas: Ediciones de la Presidencia de la República, 2001), 76–77.

28.   See "The Challenge of Sustainable Development and the Culture of Substantive Equality," my lecture delivered at the Cultural Forum of the Latin American Parliaments' "Summit on the Social Debt and Latin American Integration" held in Caracas, Venezuela, July 10–13, 2001; published in *Monthly Review* 53, No. 7 (December 2001), 10–19.

29.   Simón Bolívar, An Address of Bolívar at the Congress of Angostura (Washington, D.C.: Byron S. Adams, 1919), 34; See also Bolívar, *Selected Works,* 1:191.

CHAPTER SIX: THE IMPORTANCE OF PLANNING AND SUBSTANTIVE EQUALITY

1.   From Chapter 8 of István Mészáros, *Social Structure and Forms of Consciousness,* vol. 1: *The Social Determination of Method* (New York: Monthly Review Press, forthcoming 2010).

2.   This is how Hegel argues his indefensible case on pages 129–30 of his *Philosophy of Right:* "The universal and objective element in work lies in the abstracting process which effects the subdivision of needs and means and thereby *eo ipso* subdivides production and brings about the division of labour. . . . At the same time, this abstraction of one man's skill and means of production from another's completes and makes necessary everywhere the dependence of men on one another and their *reciprocal relation* in the satisfaction of their other needs. . . . When men are thus dependent on one another and reciprocally related to one another in their work and the satisfaction of their needs, subjective self-seeking turns into a contribution to the satisfaction of the needs of *everyone else.* That is to say, by a *dialectical advance,* subjective self-seeking turns into the *mediation* of the particular through the universal, with the result that each man in earning, producing, and enjoying on his own account is *eo ipso* producing and earning for the enjoyment of everyone else."

3.   Karl Marx, *Economic and Philosophic Manuscripts of 1844,* 111–112.

4.   MECW, vol. 5, 49.

5.   Paracelsus, *Selected Writings* (London: Routledge & Kegan Paul, 1951), 176.

6.   Paracelsus, *Leben und Lebensweisheit in Selbstzeugnissen* (Leipzig: Reclam Verlag, 1956), 134.

7.   Marx, *Economic and Philosophic Manuscripts of 1844,* 99.

8.   Ibid.

9.   Ibid., Marx's emphases.

10.   Ibid., 111–2

11. I have discussed these problems in considerable detail in my book *The Challenge and Burden of Historical Time* (New York: Monthly Review Press, 2008). See in particular Chapter 6, "Economic Theory and Politics—Beyond Capital," and Chapter 9, "Socialism in the Twenty-first Century."

12. Marx, *Economic and Philosophic Manuscripts of 1844*, 114. Marx's emphases.

13. This is how another philosophical genius, Immanuel Kant, can turn everything upside-down when his perceived class interests so demand: "The *general equality* of men as subjects in a state coexists quite readily with the *greatest inequality* in degrees of the *possessions* men have, whether the possessions consist of corporeal or spiritual superiority or in material possession besides. Hence the general equality of men also coexists with *great inequality of specific rights* of which there may be many. Thus it follows that the welfare of one man may depend to a very great extent on the will of another man, just as the *poor are dependent on the rich* and the one who is *dependent must obey* the other as a *child* obeys his parents or the *wife* her husband or again, just as one man has command over another, as one man serves and another pays, etc. Nevertheless, all subjects are equal to each other before the law which, as a pronouncement of the general will, can only be one. This law concerns the *form* and not the *matter* of the object regarding which I may possess a right." See Immanuel Kant, "Theory and Practice: Concerning the Common Saying: This May Be True in Theory But Does Not Apply to Practice," in Carl J. Friedrich, ed., *Immanuel Kant's Moral and Political Writings* (New York: Random House, 1949), 415–6.

CHAPTER SEVEN: A STRUCTURAL CRISIS OF THE SYSTEM
JANUARY 2009 INTERVIEW IN *SOCIALIST REVIEW*

1. This interview in *Socialist Review* was introduced with these words: "István Mészáros won the 1970 Deutscher Prize for his book *Marx's Theory of Alienation* and has written on Marxism ever since. He talks to Judith Orr and Patrick Ward about the current economic crisis."

CHAPTER EIGHT: THE TASKS AHEAD
MARCH 2009 INTERVIEW IN *DEBATE SOCIALISTA*

1. István Mészáros, *Beyond Capital* (London: Merlin Press, 1995), 681.

2. See the discussion in Chapter 4, "Radical Politics and Transition to Socialism," in this book, especially pages 111–116

3. Quoted in István Mészáros, *The Challenge and Burden of Historical Time* (New York: Monthly Review Press, 2008), 397.

4. See the documentation of these problems in "The Structural Crisis of Politics," Chapter 10.3, in *The Challenge and Burden of Historical Time.*

5. Quoted in ibid, 131.

6. See in this respect a most insightful book by John Bellamy Foster and Fred Magdoff, *The Great Financial Crisis: Causes and Consequences* (New York: Monthly Review Press, 2009).

7. $65 billion was the figure published the day after his trial. Earlier it was quoted as "only" $50 billion. What is, however, much more important in this matter is that the Madoff case is only the tip of the iceberg, as revealed also by the exposure of Sir Alan Stanford's fraudulent financial empire, operating primarily in Latin America. Nor is it conceivable that such monumental fraudulent ventures could be operated by a few isolated individuals. No one could at this point in time give a truly reliable figure of the sums actually involved—and covered up by all kinds of vested interests—on a global scale.

8. *Beyond Capital*, 730. In Portuguese, *Para além do capital,* (São Paulo: Boitempo, 2002), 851.

9. Fernando Silva, "Crise mundial recoloca necessidade de projeto de poder dos trabalhadores," November 25, 2008.

Index